Why does every romance novel end with the proposal, engagement, and marriage? Because that is what we all love to read about! In *True Love: Engaging Stories of Real-Life Proposals,* Eva Marie has beautifully blended exciting and romantic marriage proposals with sonnets, quotes, and traditions, emphasizing the calling the bride of Christ has on "her" life. Reading this book will bring a smile to your face and a lift to your life!

Marita Littauer
Speaker/Author
President, CLASServices Inc.

Eva Marie's new book on true love and engaging proposals is a hope chest full of wonderful and witful proposals. I loved every tender moment and blushing proposal. This is a book every bride-to-be must put on her list of "I do's!" and every husband and wife should buy for the heirloom journal pages in the back.

Linda Evans Shepherd

True Love: Engaging Stories of Real-Life Proposals is a delightful and enthralling collection of stories that will bring a tear, make you laugh, and force you to to ponder the significance of marriage.

Kathy Collard Miller,
speaker and author of
Why Do I Put So Much Pressure on Myself?

True Love

*Engaging Stories of
Real-Life Proposals*

EVA MARIE EVERSON

PROMISE
PRESS
An Imprint of Barbour Publishing

Dedicated

To my wonderful, godly husband, Dennis.
Thank you for saying, "Yes!"
And to the special gifts he has given to me:
Christopher, Ashley, and Jessica.

And to my brother…

from the Author

My good friend Heather Avery Clyde and I sat in the drama room of our church, Northland, A Church Distributed (Orlando, Florida). Though younger than I am by nearly twenty years, I felt a natural friendship with Heather and her husband, Rob. "How did you two meet?" I asked her. For the next several minutes Heather shared their beautiful love story and exciting engagement.

A few evenings later, as I stood in the parking lot of the church talking with my friend Glenn Hansen, mutual friends Dennis and Christy came running over. Christy extended her left hand and a sparkling diamond shimmered in the glow of light from the streetlamps. "He whisked me off to New York City," Christy shared. "He proposed in the most romantic way!"

I soon shared these stories with my youngest daughter. "How did Daddy propose to you?" she asked.

I laughed. "He didn't. I proposed to him. . .six times before he said yes!"

I realized then that the question that led to our marriage—one that I repeated several times between that sixth attempt and the "I do's"—had since ceased to be told. Our children have no idea as to how we came to be a married couple!

This led me to another realization. I didn't know how my parents became engaged. . .or my grandparents! I immediately got on the telephone and began investigating.

I also realized that most people rarely repeat their marriage proposal stories after the grand wedding day, yet they are some of the most fun, adventurous, and romantic stories we carry within us. A book idea was born.

What fun I have had writing this book! I am eternally grateful to all the husbands and wives who allowed me to delve into their personal lives and re-tell their stories. A special "thank-you" to the founders and staff of CLASServices, Inc. (Christian Leaders, Authors, Speakers Services) who gave the necessary tools then cheered me onward to my dream. I must extend a special thank-you to Mo and Sue Matrajt. Without their understanding and encouragement, I don't know how I would have finished this project. Naturally, I will never be able to thank Barbour Books/ Promise Press enough for the opportunity to compile these stories and share them with the world. And, of course, a heartfelt thanks to agent extraordinaire, William Watkins. Obviously, the biggest THANK-YOU goes to my heavenly Father, the Giver of all good things. . .He who truly is love.

My prayer for everyone who opens these pages is that the most beautiful and powerful proposal story ever told will be realized, for we are the bride of Christ and He is our Bridegroom.

EVA MARIE EVERSON

In the Beginning. . .

It's a magical moment. Butterflies flutter from deep within the man and woman as they gaze into each other's eyes. He could swear his Adam's apple has formed a knot. She's positive that her heart has skipped a beat. . .maybe two.

And then he asks the question she's waited her whole life to hear.

"Will you marry me?"

It wasn't always like this. There was a time when rings, flowers, fuzzy little teddy bears, and candlelit dinners were unheard of. Yet the air of excitement was the same, as it well should have been! The union of a man and woman in matrimony is the example that God the Father has given to us in reference to His Son and the church. Revelation 19:7–9 (NIV) reads, in part:

> "The wedding of the Lamb has come,
> and his bride has made herself ready.
> Fine linen, bright and clean, was given her to wear. . . .
> 'Blessed are those who are invited
> to the wedding supper of the Lamb!' "

Though we don't know the name of the man who popped the question first, we do know that marriage dates back to the beginning of Genesis. The first bride and groom were Eve and Adam; their wedding was officiated by God. But there was no "proposal" per se.

Today's society witnesses a variety of marriage proposals, and this book explores a great deal of them. From ski trips to fortune cookies, the men in these stories have endeared themselves as some of the funniest, swiftest, most adventurous, and romantic heart stealers! In the days of the ancient Hebrews, however, when marriage was one of the three most important events of a man's life ("Any Jew who has not a wife is no man." —Talmud), marriage was celebrated as the most significant. This union was a two-step process that included a dowry (*mo har*) and an engagement period (*Kiddushin*) that was so serious it was legally binding. In fact, should the marriage not take place, the bride was forced to obtain a divorce lest she not be allowed to marry any other man. Should she be found unfaithful, she was stoned to death or sent away.

The betrothal ceremony included the taking of oaths, presents to the bride, and a grand feast. That done, the bridegroom returned to his home while the new bride began a period of preparing herself or making herself ready. Though they did not live together or consummate the marriage, this man and woman (in those days she was as young as age twelve to fourteen) were bound to each other.

The time between the betrothal and the second stage of the marriage, the Marriage Proper (*Chuppah*), varied from a few days (in the earliest days of man), to a year for virgins and a month for widows. The days were busy! The groom prepared his home for the woman who would soon live there, and the bride prepared herself with the help of her friends to be a good wife and mother. Communication between the two involved a go-between. A friend of the bridegroom served as the communicator.

And then the day arrived—though no one knew for sure exactly when it would be. The groom's father said, "It's time to get your bride!" The groom slipped into his wedding garments and a nuptial crown, or turban. He, along with his friends, stepped out of his home and into the village streets. The friends cried out, "Behold! The bridegroom comes!" as they began to march toward the bride's home. People along the way heard the joyous news and began to pour into the streets. Musicians and singers joined the caravan and added to the merriment. It was now near the midnight hour.

True Love

What a beautiful sight it must have been! All along the way, lit torches cut into the black night and the joyous cries of the people alerted those who attended the bride that it was time. Friends helped her into her wedding gown and she was veiled.

Can't you imagine the hush of the crowd as she stepped out to meet her bridegroom? Every bride is beautiful! A momentary silence, followed by a cry of joy, and the wedding party turned and made its way back to the home of the groom as a feast was prepared and festivities lasting from seven to fourteen days were enjoyed.

The marriage was finally consummated when the bridal couple entered the groom's chamber where the bridal bed, covered by a canopy (*Chuppah*) awaited. This age-old custom began in the days of the patriarchs when a man would take his bride into the tent of his mother. In modern Jewish weddings, the bride and groom, along with their attendants, stand under a canopy during the ceremony.

Understanding the symbolism and ancient traditions of engagements and weddings gives Christians today a sense of the importance of Jesus' role of Bridegroom and our role as bride. He has gone to prepare a place for us. He tells us in His Word that we are to prepare ourselves for His return.

[Jesus said,] "Keep watch, because you do not know the day or the hour."   MATTHEW 25:13 NIV

Though the stories you are about to read are fun and romantic, the greatest marriage proposal you will ever hear has already been whispered in your heart. Jesus has spoken His betrothal vow to His bride and she has willingly accepted His gifts.

Meet you at the *Chuppah*. . .

11

Three words, dear Romeo, and good night indeed.
If that thy bent of love be honourable,
Thy purpose marriage, send me word tomorrow,
By one that I'll procure to come to thee,
Where and what time thou wilt perform the rite;
And all my fortunes at thy foot I'll lay,
And follow thee, my lord,
throughout the world.

WILLIAM SHAKESPEARE
Romeo and Juliet
Act II, Scene II

*This is now bone of my bones
and flesh of my flesh;
she shall be called 'woman,'
for she was taken out of man."
For this reason a man will leave his father and mother
and be united to his wife, and they will become one flesh.*

GENESIS 2:23–24 NIV

Proposals
That Make You Laugh

*G*ood evening. I'm the census man. I have to find out a few things. May I come in? Thank you. May I kiss you? Thank you. How many females in here? Three? That's good. How many males? None, huh? Oh, that's bad. Have to do something about that. . . . Can you cook? Can you sew? Can you take care of a man in the style he's not been accustomed to? Gotta know all those things before I give you a license. No, not for a dog, for the other kind. Oh, by the way. . .will you marry me?"

CARY GRANT TO CAROLE LOMBARD
In Name Only
1939, RKO Radio

Abraham was now old and well advanced in years, and the LORD had blessed him in every way. He said to the chief servant in his household. . ., "I want you to swear by the LORD, the God of heaven and the God of earth, that you will not get a wife for my son from the daughters of the Canaanites, among whom I am living, but will go to my country and my own relatives and get a wife for my son Isaac.". . .So they called Rebekah and asked her, "Will you go with this man?"

"I will go," she said. . . . Then Rebekah and her maids got ready and mounted their camels and went back with the man. So the servant took Rebekah and left. Now Isaac had come from Beer Lahai Roi, for he was living in the Negev. He went out to the field one evening to meditate, and as he looked up, he saw camels approaching. Rebekah also looked up and saw Isaac. She got down from her camel and asked the servant, "Who is that man in the field coming to meet us?"

"He is my master," the servant answered. So she took her veil and covered herself. . . . Isaac brought her into the tent of his mother Sarah, and he married Rebekah. So she became his wife, and he loved her. . . .

GENESIS 24:1–4, 58, 61–65, 67 NIV

He was my friend long before we fell in love. We knew one another over a year before we had our first official date. As I recall, this date was a shopping trip to an antique mall, something we continue to enjoy today.   EVA MARIE EVERSON

The Spy Who Loved Him

Robert and Sharon Diacheysn

Robert Diacheysn and Sharon Robinson were "best friends" for a year before they began dating. Two years later they were very much in love, seriously discussing their future together, and sincerely praying that God would confirm what they believed: that He had brought them together forever. They had even gone so far as to drive to New York's Diamond District in search of the type of engagement ring Sharon desired.

"Oh, Robert," Sharon exclaimed with a deep, throaty chuckle, pointing to a marquis solitaire, "that's the one!"

Robert took a quick peek at the price. "You sure you wouldn't like to look at a few others?"

Sharon nudged him playfully. "Not unless you want to look for another wife!"

Two days later Robert drove back into the city and purchased Sharon's heart's desire. . .well, as far as rings are concerned. His plan was to surprise Sharon on her birthday which was a couple of weeks away. What he wasn't aware of, however, was that his girlfriend was, in fact, a spy. When Robert wasn't looking, she had peeked in his day planner.

"Aha!" she said with a grin. "Planning on getting engaged on my birthday. Better get a new outfit! It's a good thing I check these things."

The traditional birthday celebration for Robert and Sharon was an evening at their favorite dinner theater in Wayne, New Jersey, where they dined and enjoyed a production of *Pippin*. Robert squirmed in his seat as he anxiously planned his proposal and noted how radiant his lady looked. In fact, he thought, her eyes never once left his. Furthermore, he began to discern that she had not left the table once all evening, not even to "powder her nose."

She knows! he thought. *The little sneak! I'll show her!*

Robert decided to postpone his surprise. As the evening wore on, Sharon's usual sweet demeanor turned to agitation. Robert grinned in victory. The show came to an end and Robert helped Sharon with her coat, escorted her to the parking lot, and opened the passenger door of his 1978 Mustang for her.

As they headed toward home, Robert popped their favorite cassette in the player. Although the two remained silent on the outside, their minds were racing on the inside!

Why didn't he propose? Sharon wondered. *Tonight was supposed to have been the night.*

Robert glanced at the clock on the dashboard. *Oh, no! It's nearly eleven-thirty. Her birthday is nearly over and I still haven't proposed! Still, I can't let her get away with her little spy job! I have to be at least one up on her!*

An idea struck Robert and he pulled the car to the shoulder of the road.

"What's wrong?" Sharon asked.

"Car sounds funny," he lied. "I told you I've been having trouble with it. I'm just gonna lift the hood and take a look-see. Just sit tight."

Robert slipped out of the car, ran around to the front, and lifted the hood. As he pretended to fiddle with the engine, a car pulled up beside him.

"Need help?" the driver asked.

"No, no! I've got it," Robert called back. The driver drove away.

Robert took a deep breath and started for Sharon's side of the car. In the few minutes he had to himself, he had decided to propose on the side of the road. "Hey, buddy! You need help?" Robert turned to see a tow truck parked beside him.

"No, thank you. I've got it."

"You sure?"

"Positive!"

The driver waved as the tow truck drove away.

"Wouldn't you know it!" Robert said through gritted teeth. "If I were really in trouble I couldn't get anyone to stop unless I threw myself in front of an oncoming car. And even that's debatable in New Jersey!"

Again, Robert took a deep breath, felt for the ring box in his pocket, and headed for Sharon's side of the car. This time he almost made it before another car pulled up beside them.

"No, thank you!" Robert called to the driver before the expected question was asked. "We're fine!" He watched the driver shake his head, then drive away.

Sharon opened her door. "What's wrong?"

Robert knelt before Sharon and, with the winter's chill sending puffs of clouds from his lips, asked the question that had been on both their minds all evening. "I have something to ask you. Will you marry me?"

Sharon threw her arms around Robert as tears began to pour down her cheeks. "Yes! Yes!"

For the next few minutes Robert held the spy who loved him. He was unwilling to break the magic of the moment, until (as he should have expected) another tow truck pulled up to the "broken-down" Mustang.

"Do you kids need help?"

"No, thank you!" they called back with a laugh.

"Everything is perfect!" Sharon exclaimed.

"Let's get outta here," Robert said. "We need to wake the folks and tell them the good news."

Robert and Sharon held hands all the way home, occasionally stealing a glance at each other. Their smiles were broad, but Robert's was perhaps a bit wider. For the first, and last, time in their lives, he had out-spied the spy.

*I*n 1477 Emperor Maximilian of Austria proposed to Mary of Burgundy by gifting her with a gold ring bedecked with diamonds. The year 1870 brought a change for non-royal brides when large amounts of diamonds were discovered in Africa. Perhaps the diamond is the most popular stone for the engagement ring because, according to ancient Greek belief, these precious gemstones' inner fire was a reflection of love's passion. Ancient Romans, however, believed that diamonds were splinters from falling stars. Regardless, more than 70 percent of betrothed women wear diamond engagement rings.

Life's Achievement

Fred and Florence Littauer

*F*lorence Chapman was in the first grade when she decided that she would be successful in life and that the way that she would be successful would be to study very hard throughout her school days. In elementary school she did everything the teachers told her to do, worked diligently at extra assignments, and received all good marks. In high school she would forego proms, football games, and other social activities, choosing to stay at home and study. When high school was but a memory, Florence had achieved high honor roll and a scholarship to attend the Massachusetts State University.

In college, Florence stayed true to her goals and dreams. She studied very hard—mostly because she had to keep her scholarship—and she worked two jobs. When she completed her courses, she graduated with a full major in English, a full major in speech, a full major in education, and a minor in psychology.

After graduation, Florence returned to her hometown, Haverhill, Massachusetts, where she accepted a job as an English and speech teacher at the local high school. She earned eighteen hundred dollars a year, with a bonus of one hundred dollars for directing the senior play. As far as Florence was concerned, she had reached her first goal. To her, the income equaled success.

Her next goal in life was to become well dressed. In order to achieve that goal, she went to Filene's Basement in Boston every weekend. Had Florence gone to the well-known department store outlet with just her paycheck, she could not have afforded to become well dressed. But in Filene's Basement a sign read: "We mark everything down 25 percent every seven days. At the end of thirty days we give our merchandise away to charity."

The very young, though very wise, Florence Chapman would go into Filene's Basement and watch a coveted item be slashed down 25 percent each week, then purchase it just before it was given away. By doing this she was able to purchase an entire wardrobe. In one year she spent her entire salary in Filene's Basement, but her closet held thirty-five dresses, thirty suits, and thirty pairs of shoes that matched. Florence Chapman declared herself the best-dressed woman in Haverhill, Massachusetts.

With her education behind her and her closet filled with beautiful clothes, Florence was now facing her next goal. Actually, it wasn't so much a goal as it was a fear. As it would be for any twenty-three-year-old English teacher living in Haverhill, Massachusetts, Florence was afraid she'd never get married.

Again, the very wise, young Florence thought the problem through. She looked around town and, in her perception, found that very few of the men in Haverhill were what she dreamed of. After all, she had worked very hard for her successes. The last thing she wanted or needed was to marry downhill.

Alas, all was not hopeless; Florence was able to narrow her

potential suitors to two men. One was a local doctor, and Florence reasoned that it would be good to marry a doctor because they make a lot of money. Being a woman who set goals and achieved them, Florence began to date the local doctor, a man with great possibilities. He was a graduate of Harvard Medical School, his father owned the local bank, he was an only child, and he was certain to inherit the family fortune.

The second available man in Haverhill was tall, dark, and handsome, but, unfortunately, he was the local priest. This, combined with Florence's years of church rearing, led her back to the local doctor, whom she dated for over a year. Yet, in that one-year period, he never once even kissed her good night. To add insult to injury, at the end of the year the doctor's father died, he chose to stop dating Florence to take care of his mother, and the local priest ran off with one of the members of his parish.

This ended Florence's quest for love in Haverhill.

The following summer, Florence went to Maine to teach drama at a girls' camp. One Friday evening, along with another counselor, Florence went to Howard Johnson's in Naples, Maine, hoping to spot what little nightlife might actually be breathing. Within moments of arriving and perching themselves outside Howard Johnson's, Florence turned to see a tall, handsome young man walking with a couple toward her. "Janice," she whispered to her companion, "don't look now, but I have spotted the best-looking thing I've seen in the woods of Maine in many a summer. What am I going to do? I can't just run over there to him! How can I meet him?"

"Smile at him!" Janice advised.

Florence smiled.

"Janice, is that you?" the young couple called out.

Hallelujah, Florence thought. *They know Janice!*

As the three greeted each other, Florence seized her opportunity.

"Hello," she said to the handsome man.

"Hi."

"I'm Florence Chapman, the drama coach at Camp Trebor where Janice is the sailing coach."

"I'm Fred Littauer."

"It's very nice to meet you, Fred. Do you live close by?"

"No, I'm from New York."

By the end of the conversation, Florence and Fred had a date for the following evening. By the end of the summer, he agreed that he would come to Haverhill so that they could continue to see each other. However, shortly after he arrived, Fred made an ominous announcement.

"I just want you to know that you are really a nice girl, but I know that I could never marry you," he said.

Well, thought Florence, *I didn't expect him to propose to me on the first date, but neither did I expect to get canceled out so quickly.* Not one to lose sight of her goals, she asked him a direct question. "What's wrong with me?"

"It's not that there's anything so wrong with you, but it's just that I'm a businessman. I have figured out how many miles it is from Larchmont, New York, to your home in Haverhill, how many miles per gallon my car gets, how much gas costs per gallon. . .I have to figure in depreciation on the car. . .lunches. . . and frankly, I'm not sure if it's worth the investment."

Florence knew that most women would have sent Fred packing after a statement like that. Not Florence. A few days later Fred had something new to report. "Ever since I told you that I couldn't marry you, you've begun to shape up! I'm thinking that if I stay a couple of more days, you may continue to improve!"

So Fred continued his visit with Florence, at the end of which Fred stated, "Let's give this six months."

A year and a half later, Fred took Florence for a ride in a horse-drawn cab in New York City's Central Park where he gave her a white orchid and a diamond ring.

The following school day, Florence gathered all her drama

pupils together and announced from the podium, "Students, Miss Chapman is getting married!"

"We can do the wedding!" the students exclaimed.

"What do you mean, do the wedding?"

"It will be like a giant senior play," one of the students filled in.

"Of course, you'll write the script!" another student added.

"And produce it!"

"And direct it!"

"And, naturally, you will have the starring role!"

The idea stuck. Florence, as she had done so many times before, began to plan.

"Elizabeth is being crowned in England," she announced to her students. "We will watch the procedures and do it better in Haverhill!" Her students gleefully agreed and soon the entire school was involved.

The household arts teacher tatted a crown. The wood shop students took broomsticks, sprayed them gold, and made scepters for the bridesmaids. Students in metal shop built racks for displaying the bridal gifts. Students in household arts planned the buffet. Every girl who had a strapless, net dress became a member of the royal court that Florence would dramatically walk through on her way to the altar. The band began warming up their rendition of the wedding march, with Florence's brother Ron at first trumpet. Finally, the students at Haverhill High School borrowed a long white Cadillac from the local shoe factory to drive Florence to and from the wedding.

As time and planning went on, one of the pupils wrote to *Life* magazine, which was doing a series called "*Life* Goes to a Party."

"Dear *Life* Magazine," she wrote, "How would you like to photograph a teacher's wedding where the pupils are doing all the work?"

Imagine the tide of emotion that rippled through Florence Chapman, Haverhill High School, and the citizens of Haverhill, Massachusetts, when *Life* magazine called Florence and said that they were going to come to her wedding and photograph it for their magazine! Sure enough, they did. The wedding of Fred and Florence Littauer was beautifully displayed and recorded in the May 18, 1953, issue of *Life* magazine.

Nearly fifty years later, Fred and Florence have three grown children, Lauren, Marita, and Fred. In 1984, they began ministering together on a full-time basis. In 1981, they formed CLASServices, Inc. (Christian Leaders, Authors, Speakers Services), a training tool that has trained, encouraged, directed, and supported thousands of Christian leaders, authors, and speakers. Additionally, Fred and Florence have written numerous books and are in high demand as speakers.

The little girl from Haverhill has been successful in business, successful in marriage and motherhood, and successful in ministry. Above all, she achieved her dream—to be successful in life.

God commanded Adam to cultivate and to keep. I believe the principle of cultivating and keeping applied not only to the Garden, but also to his relationship with Eve as well. I don't think that's ever changed for any of us. Dr. Joel Hunter

He proposed in his garage one weekend as I was doing his laundry. "I have been thinking," he said. "Let's get married." After I answered yes, he reached over and turned off the light to kiss me in the dark. Just then the bell in the clothes dryer rang. Eight years later, I remember that moment every time I do the laundry. I'll bet no other woman has such a cherished spot in her garage! Shirley Doan

True Love

Flanagan's Wake

Brian and Barbara Boswell

Brian Boswell and Barbara Loftus met in a most modern, romantic way. "If God could use a talking donkey, he could certainly use a computer!" Brian now explains to friends when asked how the happy couple ever became a twosome.

Brian, who lived in Maryland, and Barb, who lived in Pennsylvania, met in an online web site, Christian Connections. Through much prayer, daily E-mail, eventual phone calls, and an at-long-last meeting, they knew that their relationship had been fashioned by God. But dating was most often a family affair. "Going out" included grade-school basketball games, dance recitals, and family movie nights with Barbara's two daughters, Amanda, age ten, and Brianna, age seven.

One evening Brian suggested something different for Barb and himself. "Let's have a romantic night out for two," he suggested. "Just you and me."

"Sounds wonderful! What do you have in mind?"

"There's an interactive play called *Flanagan's Wake* at The Quiet Man's Pub in Philadelphia. If that sounds okay with you, I can get the tickets for next Saturday night."

"Order those tickets!"

When Saturday evening arrived, Barb placed loving kisses on the cheeks of her daughters. "Be sweet for Mommy and obey Aimee. Brush your teeth and don't forget to say your prayers." She turned to the teenage sitter. "Aimee, the number to the theater is on the kitchen counter. Don't hesitate to call if you need me."

"I won't," Aimee replied. Barb offered up a prayer that a call wouldn't come.

Flanagan's Wake audience/participants were required to wear name tags. The men's name tags were printed with their real names, followed by "Patrick"; the women's name tags were printed with "Mary," followed by their real names. On this particular Saturday evening, "Brian Patrick" and "Mary Barbara" sat chatting happily near the rear of the pub as the actors entered the auditorium from behind the audience.

"Boo-hoo," sobbed Fiona, the grieving "widow" of the poor, deceased Flanagan, as she walked toward the stage. "Oh, boo-hoo!" Stopping next to Barb's aisle seat, Fiona took Barb's arm and sniffled through her thick brogue. "No one can coomfort like a girlfriend, Mary Barbara. Coom and sit wit me, will ya?"

Wouldn't you know it! Barb thought. *I'm the first one they pick on!* But Barb decided to be a good sport. Playing along, she followed Fiona, the priest, and several other cast members to the small stage. The wake was beginning and Barb tried to look consoling at appropriate moments, but deep inside she was wishing she were sitting with Brian. After all, this was their first "grown-up" date in quite some time, and they were a good thirty feet apart!

"Mary Barbara, haf ya ever looved soomeone like I looved me Flanagan?" Fiona asked Barb, interrupting her thoughts. The two women were sitting next to each other.

"No," Barb answered, shaking her head.

"Well," she continued, "doo ya haf a special soomeone to loove?"

Nervous beyond belief, Barb again shook her head and said, "No."

Fiona's expression revealed that "Mary Barbara" was not playing along the way she was supposed to! "Tell me, Mary Barbara, did ya coom here to mourn Flanagan ahl by yerself?"

"Yes," Barb answered, the untruth slipping easily from her lips.

The priest interrupted. "Well, then, who's that over there? I saw ya wit him earlier. Is that your broother, then? Bring her broother oop here!"

Barb giggled, knowing how shy Brian was about being in front of a lot of people. The embarrassed Brian was called up to the stage. He rose from his seat, walked forward, and stood at the front of the small stage where Barb was sitting.

The priest looked at Brian with a skeptical expression. "Yer not her broother, are you?"

"No," Brian quietly shook his head.

How amusing that we've both been drawn into the play, Barb thought.

"Well, then," continued the priest, "do ya have anything to say fer yerself?"

Brian turned to Barb and grinned. In that moment, Barb knew exactly what was going to happen. She jumped to her feet as he began to go down on one knee, then gently tugged her back to sitting. Barb laughed and cried simultaneously.

"Barb," Brian said as he held her hands in his, "I truly believe that God has written your name on my heart, and I love you with everything that's in me. So I'm here to ask you if you'll marry me."

"Of course I will," she whispered as her eyes filled with tears. "I love you, Brian!"

Brian and Barbara Boswell—met on the Internet—became engaged at an Irish wake!

The wedding cake in Ireland is a fruitcake.

Thank You, Alexander Graham Bell

Dan and Bonnie Watkins

"My boyfriend is coming over for dinner this evening," Bonnie's college roommate informed her as soon as they took a snack break from their studies. Bonnie was in her junior year at the University of Texas where she was studying Oral Interpretation of Literature in the Speech Department.

"Okay," Bonnie said.

"He's bringing his roommate," the roommate continued.

"Oh, Johnette! You know I've sworn off men!" Bonnie knew exactly what Johnette was up to. Bonnie had recently ended an engagement to her high school sweetheart, and subsequent dating had not gone well.

"He's real cute and real smart. Besides, tomorrow is his birthday. We'll make spaghetti. . ."

A few hours later, when the doorbell rang, Bonnie answered it. When she opened the door and saw Dan Watkins for the first time, she thought, *I'm gonna marry this guy!*

Bonnie and Dan were immediately compatible. That first night they talked by the apartment's pool until two o'clock the next morning. The next evening, Bonnie invited Dan over for an impromptu birthday party with silly gifts. Dan followed by asking Bonnie to the park where their attempts at building a kite from newspaper failed. Laughing at their lack of accomplishment, they started what has since become their favorite expression: "But we just don't care!"

Over the next two years Dan and Bonnie spent most of their

time together. . .usually studying (they were both serious students). Then, in May 1972, Bonnie graduated. Dan had one more year to go.

"Bonnie," the chairman of the speech department said, "I must advise you to go to another school—Louisiana State University in Baton Rouge—for your graduate degree. It will, in the long run, be better for you."

Dan didn't want to hold Bonnie back either. They said their good-byes in front of Bonnie's packed-to-the-hilt '72 Vega, and Bonnie drove across the state line into Louisiana to begin classes at LSU.

Several months later Bonnie awoke early one Saturday morning. She showered and dressed, then settled in to think about the long list of things that she needed to accomplish that morning. But mostly, she was feeling sorry for herself. Bonnie missed Dan terribly and was beginning to doubt her decision to leave him.

"I'm calling him," she said to herself. "Even though he likes to sleep late, it's noon already and I need to talk with him."

Dan answered on the first ring. His muffled "hello" told Bonnie that she had, indeed, awakened him.

"Hi!" Bonnie chirped.

"Hi."

"I've got so much to do today, but I wanted to call you first. I have research to do in my boring Introduction to Graduate Studies class. It just seems so stupid to me to look these titles up! In fact, for the last few years I've thought so. And I have tons of reading. . .too much reading, if you want to know the truth. And I have papers to write." Suddenly Bonnie choked back a sob. "I miss you, Dan! I miss you terribly and I think that I just shouldn't have left! Do you miss me? Do you miss me as much as I miss you? What do you think about getting married?"

"Yeah. Sure."

Bonnie paused only briefly. She didn't want to break the flow of the moment. "Okay, then. I guess I woke you. Sorry. Go back to sleep."

"Okay."

That evening, as Bonnie was preparing her dinner, the phone rang.

"Hello?"

"Hi," Dan returned, sounding a little more awake this time. "I need to ask you something."

"Okay."

"Did you call me this morning?"

"Yeah," Bonnie answered.

"Did we talk about getting married or was that a dream?"

"We did."

"What did I say?" Dan asked.

"You said you wanted to."

"Oh, good, I was hoping that's what I said."

Memorial Day 1973, Dan, wearing military whites (he was in ROTC) met Bonnie, who wore her sister's wedding gown, at the altar in a quaint wooden chapel at Bergstrom Air Force Base.

The shirt he wore on their first date still hangs in their closet, in spite of the fact that Dan can no longer fit into it. Bonnie is, above all, a hopeless romantic.

Mary Todd's wedding ring from Abraham Lincoln was inscribed "Love is Eternal."

True Love

I was about sixteen when I met Ivey at church and he asked me if he could walk me home. We didn't really 'go together'. He'd come over to the house and stay till about eleven o'clock or so. . .until Papa would come out and say, 'It's bedtime.' Ivey would know to go!

"One Friday evening I swept the yard. I put the broom up and said, 'Next time I sweep the yard I'll be Mrs. Purvis.'

"Mama said, 'Yeah. . .'

"I said, 'Well, I will!'

"A few days later was Christmas Day 1920. Ivey and I had planned to elope that day. . . . I didn't want Papa to know because he'd tease me. I rode the jitney (a single rail car) to Mendes, Georgia and went over to Daisy Tucker's house. Daisy was a friend of mine. Her mother, Miss Katie, and I were talking about what I wanted for Christmas then Daisy and I went out for a walk. When we came back Ivey was there.

"Miss Katie said, 'Here's your Christmas present, Elma!'

"Ivey and I walked out. We went out to Johnny Bacon's house. . .out in the woods. . .and I was so embarrassed I wouldn't get out of the buggy. Johnny, who was a justice of the peace, and his wife came outside and he married us. Here we were getting married, and we'd never so much as held hands! But we were married sixty-six years before Ivey died. We had seven children, buried three, and lost two homes to fire. We had some hard times, but we honored our vows and stuck it out. Ivey's been gone since 1986, and I still miss him."

Excerpts from interviews with
ELMA D. PURVIS, GRANDMOTHER OF
EVA MARIE EVERSON

30

*M*y very dreams are yours.

DOROTHY OSBORNE
to SIR WILLIAM TEMPLE, *1653*
They married December 25, 1654.

*I will betroth you to me forever;
I will betroth you in righteousness and justice,
in love and compassion.
I will betroth you in faithfulness.*

HOSEA 2:19–20 NIV

*I miss you even more than I could have believed; and I
was prepared to miss you a good deal. . .so this letter is just
really a squeal of pain. It is incredible how essential to me
you have become. . . . But oh my dear, I can't be clever and
stand-offish with you: I love you too much for that.*

VITA SACKVILLE-WEST

He Said What?

Randy and Patti Iverson

For Randy Iverson, meeting Patti Wing was a dual event. Way back in 1967, Randy, who was in high school, was the "good church boy." His first introduction to Patti was at one of the youth functions sponsored by the church where his father was a board member and his mother was the church secretary. He was intrigued enough to want to know more about the young girl whose sister and brother-in-law were members of their congregation.

"Mom, can you give me the phone number for Patti Wing? Her sister is Bobbie Pickel," he asked his mother a few days later.

"Sure, honey. I don't think that will be a problem." Mrs. Iverson gave her son the number to Patti's home in South Pasadena, California (about forty miles from Randy's home in Covina). He immediately telephoned to ask her for a date. Unfortunately, Patti's father, a small man with a Napoleon complex and a well-earned reputation for his "cussin'," answered the phone.

"I don't know where in the **** that **** Pat is but if she doesn't get her *** home. . ."

That was enough for sweet Randy. It was some time later, after the two had graduated from high school and Patti's father had died, before the two would meet again and Randy would draw up enough nerve to call. Ironically, life had come full circle. . .back to a youth function at Evangelical Free Church.

"You're going with me to my church barbecue," Patti's eldest sister, Bobbie, informed Patti and twin sister, Peggy.

"Aaugh!" the twins moaned. "That's the last thing we want to do on a Saturday night!"

"Well, you're going and you're going to enjoy it. You could use a little church in your lives."

There were only two young men at the barbecue; one was in some sort of a body cast and the other, to Patti's way of thinking, was shy and cute. This, of course, was Randy, who was in a dilemma of his own. He couldn't decide which of the twins to hang out with.

It was Patti that Randy chose. He courted her by taking her to parks where they played like children. They toured nearby Hollywood, dined in fine restaurants, and attended the movie premieres of *Grand Prix* and *2001, A Space Odyssey*. They had a mutual enjoyment for bowling, golfing, hiking, biking, skiing, and swimming at the beach.

One starry and moonlit evening, in the summer of '71, Randy drove Patti up to the mountains of Los Angeles in his beige VW Kharmann Ghia. "Let's go check out the stars," he said. During the drive, Johnny Mathis sang the dreamy "Twelfth of Never" through the technology of the car's new FM radio, followed by The Righteous Brothers' ballad "Unchained Melody."

When the couple arrived, the mood in the VW was definitely romantic, but in a tiny car with a gearshift and a love for the Lord between them, cuddling was not possible or probable.

"Let's get out," Randy said. "We can go stand over there for a while." He pointed to a nearby area. He held Patti's hand as they walked a short distance, then stepped behind her and wrapped her in his arms. The weather was warm and balmy and Patti sighed as she leaned against Randy.

"I love you so much, Patti," Randy whispered. "I know that God has brought us together. Even though we almost missed the boat a couple of years ago, when I first met you, God had a plan and a purpose for us to come together."

Patti's head fell against Randy's shoulder. *I love you, too,* she thought. *I'm so content. . .and so sleepy. . . .*

"Look at how beautiful everything is tonight. The stars, the moon. It's perfect. We're perfect. . ."

Patti nodded and closed her eyes.

"I want to spend the rest of my life with you. . ."

Patti relaxed completely as Randy's words blended with her thoughts, becoming a blur.

". . .spending our days and nights as man and wife, doing whatever God has in mind for us." Randy remained quiet for a moment. Patti's breathing became deep and even. "Patti, will you marry me? Patti?"

Patti jerked awake. "What?"

Randy laughed. "Did you hear a word I just said?"

"I think I fell asleep. What did you say?"

"I asked you to marry me, you nut!"

Patti's eyes opened wide. "Well, I'm awake now!"

It would happen again. For exactly one year, Randy and Patti were engaged; ample time for Patti to flash her diamond and for the happy couple to reflect on the type of marriage they would have.

"God will be the focus of our lives together," Randy whispered to Patti one moonlit evening. "We'll have kids, and if God gives me the desire of my heart, I'll support us as a fireman." Patti nodded in agreement. She was listening with her ears and her heart.

But on the day of their wedding, as the pastor said, "Do you, Patti, take this man to be your lawfully wedded husband? To have and to hold, from this day forward, for better or for worse, for richer or for poorer, in sickness and in health, and forsaking all others cleave only unto him for as long as you both shall live?" Patti didn't respond. The pastor leaned over and whispered, "Patti?"

"What? Oh, I'm sorry! I was distracted by the flower girl! Could you say it again?"

It's been nearly thirty years since Randy and Patti spoke their vows. Patti is still learning to listen, and Randy is still laughing.

God never fails.

*Russian brides and grooms
give gifts to their guests, while
bridal couples in Scotland
have their feet washed by friends,
a custom performed to help them on their new path.*

After graduation Emmitt was drafted and had to go to the army. We clung to each other and cried. I watched that big Greyhound bus carry my high school sweetheart away. . .as far as I could see. Emmitt wrote faithfully during the years that he was gone. He told me of his love and how homesick he was, yet not one single time did he ever mention anything about marriage. Finally, after what seemed to be an eternity, Emmitt's tenure in the army was up. I counted the hours till I could see him. When I saw him get off the train, I gasped! He was even more handsome than ever and just being in his presence made my heart leap! But my joy turned to disappointment and dismay when he told me that he and some army buddies were going to Alaska to strike gold. I was devastated!

"Will you marry me?" I screamed. I hadn't planned to say it. In fact, I was shocked at what I heard coming out of my mouth!

Emmitt had the most surprised look on his face. Then he swooped me up in those big strong arms and said, "I thought you'd never ask!"

JOAN CLAYTON

True Love

*W*ithout love and laughter
there is no joy;
live amid love and laughter.

HORACE

∞

In the Middle of a Cornfield

Geoff and Jan Moore

*I*t was during Taylor University's Freshman Orientation Week that Geoff Moore met Jan Boberg. They had their first date before classes started and continued to date throughout their college years.

During the summer between their junior and senior years, Geoff invited Jan to visit him at his home in Texas. She accepted the invitation and on August 15, 1982, he drove to the airport and waited anxiously for her to disembark from her plane. As soon as she did and the initial greetings were out of the way, Geoff said, "Come on! Let's go say hi to the folks."

Geoff knew that this day was the day he would ask Jan to marry him—he had, in fact, already spoken to her parents—but Jan was clueless. After they arrived at his family home and Jan said her "hellos" and settled in just a bit, Geoff made another suggestion. "Want to go for a drive?"

"Sure!"

The drive was an exercise for Geoff. . .an exercise in looking for a quiet place to pop the question. When he finally found it, it was a country road in the middle of a cornfield. Geoff stopped the car, turned to Jan, and said, "Jan, I want you to know how important you are to me."

Jan narrowed her eyes slightly. *His voice is wobbling! He's going to propose!*

It took him a while to do it, but when Geoff finally got to the question, Jan answered, "Yes," then began to cry. She cried for five minutes. When she finally calmed, Geoff presented her with a ring, which caused her to cry all the more.

"Let's go to Pizza Hut to celebrate," Geoff suggested.

With a slight nod of her head, Jan answered, "Okay."

On June 18, 1983, after they had graduated from college, Geoff Moore married his college sweetheart. In 1990 he began a contemporary Christian recording career that includes eighteen top five radio singles, nine number-one hits, multiple Grammy nominations, and two Dove awards. His highest accomplishment, however, is his role as husband to Jan and father to Joshua and Justin.

If You Could See What I See

Written by GEOFF MOORE and STEVEN CURTIS CHAPMAN

All of my life, I have dreamed that somehow love would find me.
Now I can't believe you're standing here.
If beauty is all in the eye of the beholder,
Then I wish you could see the love for you that lives in me.

And you would know you have my heart
If you could see what I see.
That a treasure is what you are,
If you could see what I see.

Created to be the only one for me.
If you could see what I see.

I know there are days that you feel so much less than ideal.
Wondering what I see in you.
It's all of the light and the grace your believing me drives me to say
I promise you a faithful love forever true.

And you would know you have my heart
If you could see what I see.
That a treasure is what you are
If you could see what I see.
Created to be the only one for me.
If you could see what I see.

Then you'd understand why I fall down to my knees
And I pray my love would be worthy of
The One who gave His life so our love could be.

If you could see what I see.
If you could see what I see.
You're created to be the perfect one for me.
If you could see what I see.

True Love

The Secret

Carlus and Nita Gibson

In 1951 Carlus Gibson was a twenty-six-year-old divorced veteran of WWII. Nita Cocreham was a senior at Galena Park High School in Galena Park, Texas. Though they were ten years apart in age, and every girl in Galena Park swooned over Carlus (and his souped-up '48 Chevy Coupe with sun visor and fender skirts), his heart belonged to Nita.

They had been dating about three months when, on a moonlit drive, handsome Carlus looked at petite Nita with deep blue eyes as they waited for the Lynchburg Ferry to make its way across the Houston Ship Channel. "I want to ask you something," he began. "But first, there is something I need to tell you."

Nita's heart stopped beating as a torrent of thoughts rushed through her mind. Was he still married? Did he have children that he had never told her about? Was he ill with some sort of incurable disease? Did he want to talk about her parents' objection to her dating him, a divorced man, ten years her senior?

"Okay," Nita whispered hoarsely.

Carlus tightened his arm around her, then uttered the words Nita will never forget: "I wear false teeth."

Nita smiled sweetly. Thanks to Carlus's younger brother, Nita was already aware of his dentures. "That's all right. I don't care."

He sighed deeply, then hugged her tighter. "Will you marry me?"

It was twenty-five years before Nita saw her husband without his dentures (and that was when he was brushing them). Time has a way of changing things. After forty-seven years of marriage, four sons, two daughters, and six grandchildren, those teeth spend every night in a plastic cup in the bathroom.

*H*e who finds a wife finds what is good and receives favor
from the LORD.   PROVERBS 18:22 NIV

∞

"Wirst Du Heiraten Mir?"

Dave and Kirstin Shafer

*D*ave Shafer was a ham radio operator in Oxford, Alabama, in
1980. One evening he turned his antenna toward Europe.
Within a few minutes he heard the familiar Morse code signal
"C Q D X; C Q D X. D L 9 H H." Little did he know that
this signal would forever change his life.

The signal Dave heard is an invitation to "talk" to someone in
a location different from the sender's location. "C Q" is always
followed by the sender's country of origin. The "D L" told Dave
that the invitation was coming from Deutschland (Germany).
Dave responded to the call.

Peter, the young man from Germany, and Dave had the typical Morse code conversation. They exchanged names, addresses,
radio signal quality, and the radio equipment that each was using.

Protocol dictates that foreign calls be logged and cards
exchanged as proof of the contact. Therefore, as is typical, Dave
and Peter logged the conversation. Dave waited in Alabama for
the card that would come from Germany. When it finally
arrived, there was included a note from Peter's eighteen-year-
old girlfriend, Kirstin.

"I am a stamp collector," she wrote. "Would you send me a
nice American stamp?"

Dave obliged Kirstin's request and in so doing began a

seventeen-year pen pal friendship with the young German girl, who, incidentally, was partially deaf.

It was nine years before Dave and Kirstin would meet face-to-face. Dave went to Germany on vacation and arranged to meet Kirstin at the end of the trip, in a rest area just off the autobahn in Hamburg. A year later Kirstin made her first trip to the United States. She visited Dave, then in 1994 she visited again.

In 1995 Dave and Kirstin's four to five letters per year increased dramatically. Responding to an invitation, Dave returned to Germany where he and Kirstin had their official first date. During the trip, Kirstin introduced Dave to her family and friends. The relationship began to blossom.

The months that followed were difficult as far as dating went. "Dating" was limited to written correspondence and phone calls. But letters took two to three weeks to cross the great wide ocean, and by that time current news was old news.

"I have an idea," Kirstin told Dave during a phone call. "Let's purchase fax machines. That way, we can fax each other every day."

"Great idea, Kirs," Dave replied. The fax machines were immediately purchased and the daily faxes began. Because of the six-hour time difference, Dave's fax would arrive just as she was getting out of bed. Some days, when he was lucky, she'd answer the phone before the faxes connected. . .just enough time to say, "I love you." Several times a week, however, Dave needed to hear Kirstin's voice a little longer, so he'd couple the fax with a voice call.

"I just saw *Moonstruck*," Kirstin wrote to Dave. "I thought this movie was very funny, especially the marriage proposal in the beginning. In this movie, Danny Aiellos wants to ask Cher to marry him. He decides to do this in an Italian restaurant he frequents. He is all set and has the waiter in on it, too. During the dinner, he comes right out and asks Cher to marry him. Cher thinks that his proposal is a bit too informal, so she tells him to get down on his knee. But this is not enough for her. She asks, 'Where is the ring?' This caught him off guard because he didn't buy her a ring. He thinks it is not necessary, even though all the customers in the restaurant tell him that yes, it is. Cher sees that he is wearing a pinkie ring and tells him to give it to her. He tells her that this was his mother's ring and he does not want to give it to her, even just temporarily. But Cher insists! So he grudgingly gives it to her. Now Cher is satisfied. . .bring on the music and the dessert!"

A few weeks later Dave wrote back. "I rented *Moonstruck*. You're right. It was very funny!" Dave also wrote that he planned to return to Germany. What he didn't write was that he would be making a quick trip to the local library to brush up on his German.

Soon, Dave was sitting in JFK Airport, awaiting departure to Hamburg, silently repeating the words he had taught himself: "Wirst du heiraten mir?" ("Will you marry me?") Knowing that there are things you can't learn about sentence structure from a book, when he spotted several women waiting for the flight to Hamburg, he thought seriously about asking them if his German was correct.

I can hear them speaking German behind me, he thought. *Should I ask them to help me? No, Shafer, you idiot! You'd just mess it all up, and they would think that you were asking them to marry you! Scratch that idea. . .you'll just have to go it alone.*

During the flight to Hamburg, Dave went over his plan. He had the ring, he had the Italian restaurant, he had the girl, and he had the desire to marry her. Best of all, he had the words. . . or so he thought.

The big night finally arrived! "Let's go out to eat tonight," Dave suggested innocently enough. "How about Italian?"

"We can go to my favorite Italian restaurant," Kirstin responded in her usual excited way. "I go there all the time."

But the restaurant was far too crowded, unlike the restaurant in *Moonstruck*. Dave and Kirstin had to share a table with another couple—strangers to them—and their conversation was nearly inaudible for a hearing person, but for Kirstin it was impossible.

The last thing I'm going to do is shout my proposal, Dave thought. *When I take her back to her apartment, I'll ask her.*

Wirst du heiraten mir. . .wirst du heiraten mir. . .wirst du heiraten mir? Dave sat on Kirstin's sofa, nervously running the big question over and over in his mind while the young German woman freshened up in the bathroom. Moments later, she came into the living room, sat next to him, and put her head on his shoulder. "Whatcha wanna do?" she asked.

"Let's just sit here and talk. I have something I want to ask you, but I want to try to ask it in German."

"Okay."

Dave took a deep breath. "Wirst du heiraten mir?"

What followed was an extremely long period of silence. *Uh-oh,* Dave thought. *Maybe I should have asked those ladies at JFK for help. . .*

More silence. *Maybe I've offended her. . .what could she possibly be thinking of me now? Have I messed up, or what?*

More silence. *Boy, Dave, you really did it this time.*

"I've often wondered what I'd say if you asked me this," Kirstin finally responded.

More silence. *Okay. . .at least I know I asked correctly.*

"If I say that I will marry you, will you promise me something?"

"Yes. What is it?"

"If I say 'yes,' will you give me plenty of time to assure myself that this is the right thing to do? You must understand that what you are asking requires me to leave everything I have known my whole life."

"Absolutely." *Okay, Kirstin. Tell me to get down on my knees.*

Nothing. *How could I have planned and planned, and anticipated so much, yet now it seems to be fizzling out?*

43

"What's wrong?" Kirstin asked.

"You didn't tell me to get down on my knees."

"Oh, my goodness!" Kirstin sprang to her feet, ran across the room to where a clock hung on the wall, set it back fifteen minutes, went back in the bathroom and shut the door.

Dave knew what the playful Kirstin was doing. She was pretending that the last fifteen minutes had never happened. The bathroom door opened, she walked out, sat next to Dave on the sofa, laid her head against his shoulder, and said, "Whatcha wanna do?"

"Let's just sit here and talk. I have something I want to ask you, but I want to try to ask it in German."

"Okay."

Again Dave took a deep breath. "Wirst du heiraten mir?"

"On your knees," she grinned.

Dave quickly came off the sofa and went down on one knee. "Wirst du heiraten mir?"

"Well, where's the ring?"

Dave pulled the ring case from his pocket and handed it to her.

Slowly Kirstin opened the box and gasped. "You silly, silly man," she whispered. "I have never seen anything so beautiful."

It was some time later before Dave knew the truth about his German proposal. Because the German language doesn't structure sentences in the same way as English sentences, he should have said, "Wirst du mir heiraten?" (Will you me marry?)

Not that it matters. In any language, the answer to the question was "Yes!" Twenty-two months later, in a lovely ceremony in Longwood, Florida, Kirstin became Mrs. Dave Shafer.

In Germany the classic engagement ring is your future wedding band: a plain, golden band with the engagement date engraved inside. During the engagement, the ring is worn on the left ring finger. Just before the wedding, the bride gives the ring to the groom's best man, who, in turn, gives it to the groom during the ceremony. The ring is placed on the bride's right ring finger. After the wedding, the ring is engraved with the wedding date.

I marry you with my eyes wide open.
You have helped me let go of the past and embrace the future.
Thank you for making me laugh again.
Bless you for taking my hand as I begin anew.

Contemporary vow for remarriage from
The Bride's Little Book of Vows and Rings
CLARKSON N. POTTER, INC.

Happiness is not having what you want.
It's wanting what you have.

UNKNOWN

I pretty much knew the night Shane was going to ask me to marry him. He is not a planner, so for him to tell me to be ready (and in a nice dress) at a certain time. . .that pretty much tipped me off. He picked me up as planned, and he drove a Jeep that had one of those "auto-lock and unlock" buttons and a "panic" button. Well, when we got to the restaurant, we got out of the car, and in front of the whole place, Shane hit the panic button (instead of the lock button) and the car lights started flashing and the horn started blowing! It was a great laugh! Dinner was really yummy. . . I'd never eaten so slowly and Shane had never eaten so fast! Usually we share a bite from the other's plate, but after I had taken the first bite of mine, I looked at his plate and he was already done! He waited until after dinner, but before dessert, to ask me. What a romantic! He got down on his knee and said all the right things. I said, "Okay!" and everyone started clapping! The maître d' brought a dozen roses and we were the stars of the restaurant! DR. HOLLY JOHNSON

Keeping the Secret

Paul and Linda Evans Shepherd

*I*f there's one thing I know, Jodie," Linda Evans said emphatically to her best friend, "it's that look lovelorn men have just before they're about to pop the question. I think I've done pretty well spotting them and then avoiding them. I'm going to finish college and then I'm off to graduate school. No man, no matter how lovesick, is going to change that."

"What about Paul?"

Paul Shepherd, a college senior at Lamar University in Beaumont, Texas, in 1978 had been Linda's friend for two years before they had begun dating. A year later as Paul neared graduation and Linda completed her junior year at the same university, Jodie's question wasn't too absurd.

"I haven't seen the look yet, so I'm sure I'm okay. Besides, Paul knows my plans."

With those words, Linda dismissed the idea, until the afternoon she drove her school bus-yellow Maverick to the library where she planned to do a little research. She caught a glance of friends who were recently engaged. Their engagement seemed so unexpected. *But,* Linda thought, *Caroline's fiancé is a college senior like Paul. The thoughts of graduation must have been enough to make him think of tying the knot.*

Suddenly, the idea that Paul could soon ask her hand in marriage seemed a real possibility. "Oh, my goodness!" she exclaimed to no one. Then she shook her head slightly as her breath caught in her throat. *No, he wouldn't ask just yet,* she thought. *Besides, it's only a week before my twenty-first birthday; if he's planning to ask me, he'll at least wait till then.*

She released her breath. "I won't worry about it now. My birthday is a whole week away. I'll worry about it later."

Later came sooner than Linda had expected. That very night, as she and Paul snuggled together on her mother's ivory and green floral sofa, Paul softly said, "I've been thinking. . ."

"Hmmmm?"

"I'm going to be an engineer. That will be a dull, tedious lifestyle. I need someone like you who will add personality and fun to my life. I love you, Linda. Will you marry me?"

Linda's eyes registered the "doe in the headlights" look before she stammered out her answer. "I can't tell you just yet. . . I love you," she added quickly. "I just need time to think." It wasn't the answer Paul had expected to receive.

True Love

"Mom, Paul asked me to marry him last night." Linda sat at the kitchen table completing schoolwork while her mother worked busily at the nearby counter.

Mrs. Evans immediately stopped her task and sat in the chair nearest Linda's. "How did you answer him?"

"I said I needed time to think! I'm having so much fun in college, Mom! I want to go to graduate school. . ."

"But?"

"But my heart knows my answer. I'll say, 'yes.' I really never had any doubt about that. I just need time to think the whole thing through."

"I'm confident of one thing, Linda," Mrs. Evans said with a pat on her daughter's hand. "You'll do the right thing."

"Thanks, Mom. Don't say anything to anybody, okay?"

"Of course not."

A week went by before Paul asked again, this time with one knee bent on the sea foam green carpet of her mother's living room. "Linda. . ."

The ringing of the telephone interrupted Paul's words. Linda and Paul looked silently into each other's eyes. Within seconds Linda's mother called out from the next room. "Linda, it's Jodie Ann. She wants to talk to you."

Paul sighed deeply and bowed his head. Linda spoke softly. "I'll just tell her to call back," she said as she reached for the nearby receiver.

"Hi, Jodie," Linda said quietly.

"Linda, I hear you're engaged!"

Linda smiled slightly, then looked deeply into Paul's eyes as he raised his head to look at her. "No, not yet."

"What? But your mother told my mother!"

Linda rolled her eyes and bit her bottom lip. Linda was sure that her mother had meant well. She should have known that "don't tell anyone" would not include Jodie's mother. After all, her mother and Jodie's mother were best friends, same as Linda

48

and Jodie. "Well. . .can I call you back?"

"Why won't you tell me now?" Jodie pleaded.

"I just can't talk!"

Linda said good-bye, replaced the receiver, and then Paul took her hand in his. "Linda, I love you, I want you to be my wife. Will you marry me?"

Linda threw her arms around him and smothered his face with kisses. "Yes!. . .Yes!. . .Yes!"

It was several hours later before Linda returned Jodie's call. "Jodie, I'm sorry I seemed so rude. Paul was in the middle of asking me to marry him when you called!"

"Oh!"

"I had to tell him before I told you."

Jodie laughed. "I see your point."

Nearly one year later, in May 1979, Linda Evans stepped into her long, white lace wedding gown and reached for her bouquet of pink roses. At the altar of the First Baptist Church in Beaumont, Paul, clad in a white tux, waited patiently as each of Linda's bridesmaids stepped up the aisle and prepared the way for his bride.

Life with Paul has been anything but boring. In addition to being an engineer, Paul pilots his own private plane and has climbed all fifty-two fourteen-thousand-foot peaks in their home state of Colorado. Linda kept her end of the bargain by adding her own touch of "personality and fun" to Paul's life as well as the lives of their two kids by keeping busy as the Christian author of eleven books and as an in-demand speaker for women's conferences around the country. "It may have taken me a while to say 'yes!' to Paul's proposal," Linda recently reported to a friend, "but I'm certainly glad I did."

Love is patient, love is kind.
It does not envy, it does not boast, it is not proud.
It is not rude, it is not self-seeking,
it is not easily angered,
it keeps no record of wrongs.
Love does not delight in evil
but rejoices with the truth.
It always protects, always trusts,
always hopes, always perseveres.
Love never fails. . . .

1 CORINTHIANS 13:4–8 NIV

The Preacher's Wife

Rev. Van and Judy Gale

Van Gale walked his date to the front door of her home. They had just gone to dinner and then to see the movie *Always*. "I really enjoyed the movie, Van," fifty-one-year-old Judy Flynn said.

"Me, too. It's one for touching the heart, isn't it?"

"Mmmm. . .," Judy agreed as they reached her door. As she opened the door and walked inside, she continued. "When I was a child, we went to a lot of movies and plays. I've always enjoyed them." She turned to look at her date, a man who also happened to be her pastor.

"Not in my home! I was raised without movies and certainly without dancing. I'm here to tell you that I had very strict parents."

True Love

There was momentary silence in the living room before Van added, "Judy, I love you."

"Van, I love you."

"Will you marry me?"

"Yes," Judy answered, then politely added, "Will you give me my first kiss?"

Van grinned, reached for Judy, and then wrapped her in his embrace. A moment passed before he moved to kiss her.

He missed!

"Can we do that again?" Judy asked sheepishly. The tension of the moment was broken as they laughed, then tried again. This time, success!

In spite of the humor surrounding their engagement, their touching story actually began thirty years before in 1967.

"Thirteen Club" was the Sunday school class for adults between the ages of twenty and thirty-three at College Church in Wheaton, Illinois. A young couple, Judy and Joe Flynn, were members of the class, along with Van Gale, who had grown up in the church. The class was filled with a lot of young couples who had children of nearly the same ages. There they enjoyed wonderful years. They had potluck dinners and often exchanged baby-sitting favors. No one had a lot of money or expensive homes. No one owned anything fancy. They simply worked together toward learning to love the Lord and each other.

Idyllic years passed before tragedy struck the Flynns. Joe contracted viral encephalitis and spinal meningitis simultaneously. The illness endured for three long months, five weeks of which he was in a coma. In 1976 Van, by this time the Reverend Van Gale, had founded Praise Fellowship Church in Carol Stream, Illinois. The Flynns were members of the church and, as their pastor when Joe passed away, Van helped Judy and her three grown children plan the funeral, pick the music selections, and then preached the service.

51

Van called regularly during the time that Judy was a new widow.

"Judy, is there anything you need? Anything I can do for you?"

"Thank you, Pastor Van," Judy answered. "You have no idea how much I appreciate your friendship."

Several years passed. Periodically Van and Judy enjoyed Sunday dinner together. Soon they found themselves enjoying each other's company more and more. For Judy, after years of being single, it was a precious time of learning to trust and love again. But there were no thoughts of marriage!

God was at work, however. Sometimes Van would say to Judy, "You know. . .a church needs a mother and the pastor needs a wife. After all, the church is a family. In the case of Praise Fellowship, it's a family without a wife or a mother. It's difficult to be a single pastor, and it's better for the church if the pastor can minister with a wife beside him. . .better for social functions, home visits, and caring ministries."

Was he hinting? Judy wondered. Or was he simply speaking the truth?

The night in her living room in September 1990, Van's question answered Judy's. In March 1991, the two services of Praise Fellowship were combined as the pastor took a wife, the "family" received a mother, and joyous cheers rang out in celebration.

In the days of slavery, African-American couples were not legally allowed to marry. Many times the wedding ceremony included jumping over a broom. Today, some African-Americans perform this symbolic rite just before the reception.

I Love You Beary Much

Tom and Melody Rabenberg

Melody Hunt and her daughter, eighteen-year-old Stephanie, pulled into the driveway of their home late Friday afternoon. It was February 12, 1993. Melody had spent the day at work, gifting the Rice Krispies teddy bears she and Stephanie had made the night before. This was a fun tradition between mother and daughter—Melody and Stephanie forming the bears in a mold, decorating them with icing and candy, then slipping them into plastic bags sealed tightly with red bows—but tiring all the same.

"What's that on the front porch?" Melody asked as she brought the car to a stop and switched off the ignition.

"Looks like a box, Mom."

"It's probably another gift for the new baby across the street. I think we've gotten more of his gifts than he has," Melody teased. "Would you mind running it across to them in a little bit?"

Mother and daughter stepped out of the car as Stephanie answered, "No, I don't mind." Melody reached into the backseat of her car and pulled out a box of leftover bears.

When the two women reached the porch, however, Melody immediately noticed that the card on the box had her name on it. "It's for me!"

"It's from the Vermont Teddy Bear Company," Stephanie noted.

"Grab it, will you, honey? I'll bet Tom has sent me a teddy bear for Valentine's Day."

Stephanie giggled. "Aaaah!"

Inside their home, Melody remarked, "How sweet of him!" as she placed the box and her purse on a nearby table.

"Open it, Mom!" Stephanie urged. Melody began to tear

into the package. Inside of the box was an adorable teddy bear with a large red bow tied around his neck. As Melody gently lifted him, she noticed that he held an envelope between his fuzzy, light brown paws.

"Oh, Stephanie, look at this. A card!"

"Hurry, Mom! Read it!"

Melody complied. " 'Dear Melody, I love you and want to spend the rest of my life with you. Will you'—oh, my goodness!—'Will you please marry me?' "

"AHHHHHHHHH!" Melody and Stephanie screamed in unison.

"Mom! Did you expect this?"

"No! I had no idea!" The women screamed again. It was then that they noticed a small gold box resting at the bottom of the package.

"Mom, it's an engagement ring! I'll bet it is!"

Melody opened the box to reveal two small chocolate truffles.

"Mom, the ring is in one of those truffles! Bite into them, Mom!"

Melody laughed. "These truffles are pretty small, Stephanie! My ring better be bigger than that!"

Stephanie laughed, too. Melody moved to the back of the house and toward a window. "I wouldn't be surprised if Tom isn't back here watching us," she said, peeking out the window. "No, no. He's not out here."

Stephanie had moved next to her mother and was peering out the window with her. "Try to call him at work."

Indeed, Tom was at work. When he answered his phone, Melody screamed, "Yes!"

They married three months later.

An Honest Valentine

Thank you for your kindness,
Lady fair and wise.
Though love's famed for blindness,
Lovers—hem! for lies.
Courtship's mighty pretty,
Wedlock a sweet sight—
Should I (from the city,
A plain man, Miss—) write,
Ere we spouse-and-wive it,
Just one honest line,

Could you e'er forgive it,
Pretty Valentine?

Honey-moon quite over,
If I less should scan
You with eye of lover
Than of mortal man?
Seeing my fair charmer
Curl hair spire on spire,
All in paper armor,
By the parlor fire;
Gown that wants a stitch in
Hid by apron fine,
Scolding in her kitchen,—
O fie, Valentine!

True Love

Should I come home surly
Vexed with fortune's frown,
Find a hurly-burly,
House turned upside down,
Servants all a-snarl, or
Cleaning steps or stair:
Breakfast still in parlor,
Dinner—anywhere:
Shall I to cold bacon
Meekly fall and dine?
No—or I'm mistaken
Much, my Valentine.

What if we should quarrel?
—Bless you, all folks do:—
Will you take the war ill
Yet half like it too?
When I storm and jangle,
Obstinate, absurd,
Will you sit and wrangle
Just for the last word—
Or, while poor Love, crying,
Upon tiptoe stands,
Ready plumed for flying—
Will you smile, shake hands,
And the truth beholding,
With a kiss divine
Stop my rough mouth's scolding?
Bless you, Valentine!

If, should times grow harder,
We have lack of pelf,
Little in the larder,
Less upon the shelf;

True Love

Will you, never tearful,
Make your old gowns do,
Mend my stockings, cheerful,
And pay visits few?
Crave nor gift nor donor,
Old days ne'er regret,

Seek no friend save Honor,
Dread no foe but Debt;
Meet ill-fortune steady,
Hand to hand with mine,
Like a gallant lady,—
Will you, Valentine?

Then, whatever weather
Come, or shine, or shade,
We'll set out together,
Not a whit afraid.
Age is ne'er alarming,—
I shall find, I ween,
You at sixty charming
As at sweet sixteen:
Let's pray, nothing loath, dear,
That our funeral may
Make one date serve both, dear,
As our marriage day.
Then, come joy or sorrow,
Thou art mine,—I thine.
So we'll wed to-morrow,
Dearest Valentine.

DIANA MARIA MULOCK CRAIK

True Love

God's Ordained

Dr. Billy and Ruth Graham

One Sunday evening after church, I walked into the parlor of the Gerstung home, where I was rooming, and collapsed into a chair. That dear professor of German and his wife, with three young boys of their own, were getting accustomed to my moods and always listened patiently. This time I bemoaned the fact that I did not stand a chance with Ruth. She was so superior to me in culture and poise. She did not talk as much as I did, so she seemed superior in her intelligence, too. "The reason I like Ruth so much," I wrote home to Mother, "is that she looks and reminds me of you."

By now I had directly proposed marriage to Ruth, and she was struggling with her decision. At the same time, she encouraged me to keep an open mind about the alternative of my going to the mission field. She was coming to realize, though, that the Lord was not calling me in that direction.

One day I posed a question to Ruth point-blank. "Do you believe that God brought us together?"

She thought so, without question.

"In that case," I said, "God will lead me, and you'll do the following."

She did not say yes to my proposal right then and there, but I knew she was thinking it over.

A test of our bond came when her sister Rosa was diagnosed as having tuberculosis. Ruth dropped out of school in the middle of my second semester to care for her. Rosa was placed in a hospital in New Mexico, and Ruth stayed with her the next fall, too.

That summer I returned home and preached in several churches in the South. Ruth's parents had returned from China on a furlough—actually, the Japanese had invaded the mainland, so the Bells were not sure if they could ever return—and had settled temporarily in Virginia, their home state.

While I was in Florida, preaching in Dr. Minder's church, I got a thick letter from Ruth postmarked July 6, 1941. One of the first sentences made me ecstatic, and I took off running. "I'll marry you," she wrote.

When I went back to my room, I read that letter over and over until church time. On page after page, Ruth explained how the Lord had worked in her heart and said she felt He wanted her to marry me. That night I got up to the pulpit and preached. When I finished and sat down, the pastor turned to me.

"Do you know what you just said?" he asked.

"No," I confessed.

"I'm not sure the people did, either!"

After I went to bed, I switched my little lamp on and off all night, rereading that letter probably another dozen times.

At the close of a preaching series just after that at Sharon Presbyterian Church in Charlotte, those dear people gave me, as I recall, an offering of $165. I raced right out and spent almost all of it on an engagement ring with a diamond so big you could almost see it with a magnifying glass! I showed it off at home, announcing that I planned to present it to Ruth over in Montreat in the middle of the day. But daytime was not romantic enough, I was told.

Ruth was staying part of that summer at the cottage of Buck Currie and his wife, whom she called uncle and aunt, and their niece, Gay. Buck was the brother of Ed Currie, one of Ruth's father's fellow missionaries in China. Their house on Craigmont Road in Black Mountain was built near a stream and had swings that went out over the water.

As I turned off the main road and drove toward the house, which was some distance off, I saw a strange creature walking down the road. She had long, straight hair sticking out all over, an awful-looking faded dress, bare feet, and what looked to be very few teeth. I passed her by, but when I suddenly realized it was Ruth playing a trick on me—her teeth blacked out so that she looked toothless—I slammed on brakes. She got in and we went on to the Currie house deep in the woods.

I had the ring with me.

We went up to what is now the Blue Ridge Parkway. The sun was sinking on one side of us and the moon rising on the other. I kissed Ruth on the lips for the first time. I thought it was romantic, but she thought, or so she told me later, that I was going to swallow her.

"I can't wear the ring until I get permission from my parents," she said apologetically.

They were away, so she sent them a telegram: "Bill has offered me a ring. May I wear it?"

"Yes," they wired back, "if it fits."

Reprinted from
Just As I Am, The Autobiography of Billy Graham
HARPERCOLLINS/ZONDERVAN, 1997

A Perfect Fit

Spence and Kathie Clarke

Kathie knew that her mother and father would like the man she had been dating. "I've been waiting a long time for someone like Spence," she told her parents on the phone one evening.

"Oh, honey, I'm excited for you," Kathie's mother exclaimed. "I know you have prayed for someone who was just right."

"He has a great sense of humor, too," Kathie went on. "That's high on my list of priorities, and Mom, dating Spence is different in that we don't do the worldly kind of dating; we'd rather allow the Lord to turn our friendship into something deeper. We enjoy just doing things together."

A few evenings later, as Spence and Kathie were preparing to go out to dinner, Spence brought out a small velvet box that held an engagement ring. "Will you marry me?" he asked.

Without a moment's hesitation, Kathie exclaimed, "Yes!"

"Let's go celebrate," Spence said with a big grin.

Kathie paused briefly. "Wait, I've got to tell Mom the good news first," she said, grabbing the phone.

Kathie's mother was so excited she blurted out, "Why don't you come over here for dinner? It won't take long to fix something. We want to meet him."

Spence agreed that it would be good to meet them. "I might even ask them for your hand," he joked.

In the car Kathie told Spence a little about her parents. "They are wonderful, Spence, very real and unpretentious."

As Kathie had expected, her parents were warm and gracious. She was surprised, however, to note that in such a short amount of time they had laid out an elegant table with their very best china and silver.

Another surprise was to come. After serving the vegetable dishes, her mother brought out a strange-looking meat dish. Kathie's eyes widened in disbelief. Her mother was serving chicken necks covered with barbecue sauce. Spence dug in and began eating as if he ate chicken necks every day of the week.

When she cornered her mother in the kitchen, she whispered, "Why in the world did you serve chicken necks?"

Blushing, Mrs. Coger confessed. "I had been cooking them for the dog. When you said you were coming right over, I realized I didn't have any meat for dinner, so I just poured barbecue sauce on them and hoped they would taste good."

Just then, they overheard Kathie's father asking Spence to pass something and then adding, "By the way, I have to know one thing. Can you fix plumbing? Kathie is always getting something plugged up and I want my son-in-law to be able to fix plumbing."

Spence laughed and said, "Yes, I have fixed a few pipes in my day. Does that qualify me?"

Later that night, as Spence was driving Kathie home, she confessed that she had been a little embarrassed about the dinner. Spence just laughed. "Your folks are great. I love them. Your dad's question was pretty funny, too."

Kathie reached across the seat, took his hand, and said with a grin, "You're going to fit into my family just fine!"

Twenty-one years later, it's still true.

There is an obvious difference (though the world may not see it) between the Christian proposal of marriage and the secular proposal of marriage. Yes, the words may be just as romantic, the setting just as creative, the ring just as exquisite. But the difference lies in the understanding of the magnitude of the union. Years ago I read two articles describing the marriage proposals of two sets of celebrities. One couple had lived together for some time, and while their proposal story was interesting and fun, it lacked something. . . . The other couple was John Tesh and Connie Selleca. The story was beautifully romantic (in my way of thinking) and their love for Christ and each other was evident throughout the piece. It was a story I would not only remember, it would be a cornerstone for writing this book.

While preparing the manuscript, I was blessed with the

opportunity to interview John about his special evening. He told me he had planned to have fireworks set off over the water in Carmel, California, where he and Connie stood on the deck outside a restaurant. Everything went as hoped, but he had not anticipated the fact that the fireworks would cause car alarms to go off and neighborhood dogs to bark. The romantic moment became quite funny when he was forced to scream his proposal rather than speak it. Regardless, Connie said "yes" and they have been happily married since 1992.

When my phone conversation with John was complete, I was left with the undeniable feeling that romance and laughter really do make the best combination! My prayer for Mr. and Mrs. Tesh is that their love and laughter never end. EVA MARIE EVERSON

Later I passed by, and when I looked at you and saw that you were old enough for love, I spread the corner of my garment over you and covered your nakedness. I gave you my solemn oath and entered into a covenant with you, declares the Sovereign LORD, and you became mine. EZEKIEL 16:8 NIV

I am your servant Ruth," she said.
"Spread the corner of your garment over me,
since you are a kinsman-redeemer."
So Boaz took Ruth and she became his wife.

RUTH 3:9, 4:13 NIV

Brides born in January may choose garnet engagement rings.
Garnets symbolize eternal friendship.

Brides born in February may choose amethyst engagement rings.
Amethysts symbolize faithfulness and sincerity.

Brides born in March may choose aquamarine engagement rings.
Aquamarines symbolize intelligence and courage.

Brides born in May may choose emerald engagement rings.
Emeralds symbolize domestic harmony and success in love.

Brides born in June may choose pearl engagement rings.
Pearls symbolize health and longevity.

Brides born in July may choose ruby engagement rings.
Rubies symbolize love and contentment.

Brides born in August may choose peridot engagement rings.
Peridots symbolize strength.

Brides born in September may choose sapphire engagement rings.
Sapphires symbolize truth and faithfulness.

Brides born in October may choose opal engagement rings.
Opals symbolize hope.

Brides born in November may choose topaz engagement rings.
Topaz symbolizes fidelity.

Brides born in December may choose turquoise engagement rings.
Turquoise symbolizes prosperity.

PROPOSALS
IN THE BLINK OF AN EYE

Love's Philosophy

The fountains mingle with the river,
And the rivers with the ocean;
The winds of heaven mix forever,
With a sweet emotion;
Nothing in the world is single;
All things by a law divine
In one another's being mingle—
Why not I with thine?

PERCY BYSSHE SHELLEY

As a young man marries a maiden, so will your sons marry you; as a bridegroom rejoices over his bride, so will your God rejoice over you. ISAIAH 62:5 NIV

I proposed that we marry. . .about six times before he agreed! After the sixth attempt he said, "Let's go get dinner." Dinner was a hot dog at Hardees. (Just call us Mr. and Miss Romantic!) Later we walked inside the Albany Mall, Albany, Georgia. We stepped into a jewelry store. I went to the left showcase; he went to the right. After a moment or two of looking at necklaces, I walked up behind him, stood on my tiptoes, and peered over his shoulder. "What are you looking at?" I asked.

"Wedding rings," he answered.

"How come?" I teased.

"If we're getting married, we'll need rings," he replied.

"Is that a proposal?" (I should have been insulted, but I wasn't.)

"The best one you're gonna get." I returned those words with a grin. Sarcasm and a smile, these were the ingredients of my marriage proposal. EVA MARIE EVERSON

One Week to Build His World

Dr. Michael and Audrey Guido

In the spring of 1943, Michael Guido was on staff at Moody Bible Institute in Chicago, Illinois.

"Michael, we need for you to go to Metter, Georgia, to conduct a revival meeting," he was instructed.

"Well, okay. . .," Michael returned reluctantly. Metter was such a small community, practically in the middle of nowhere! Up until then, he had enjoyed meetings with large attendance records in cities such as Chicago and Cleveland. But Michael was obedient to his calling and he packed his bags.

Services began on Sunday morning, and the rural Georgia church was packed to capacity. A few days into the meeting, several students from Metter High School approached the superintendent of schools. "We've been going to the revival meetings," they said, "and we'd like for Mr. Guido to come and speak at an assembly!"

"I've heard him, too!" the superintendent replied. "And I think that's a wonderful idea!"

The next day the twenty-eight-year-old traveling evangelist arrived at the school and was walking down the hall with the superintendent when suddenly they stopped. The superintendent said, "I have a teacher I'd like for you to meet. She's very smart. . .in fact, she has been accepted at Johns Hopkins after finishing her pre-med. She's brilliant. She's beautiful. But she's also an agnostic. I wish you would lead her to the Lord."

Just then that teacher came down the hall. The principal

stopped the lovely young woman. "Miss Forehand, I want you to meet this preacher."

Audrey Forehand stuck up her nose and replied, "I don't care to meet any preacher!"

Michael was quick to respond. "But Miss Forehand, I want to meet you!"

"Why?"

"Because I want you to become a Christian."

Audrey stamped the floor. "There is no God!"

Michael opened his Bible to Psalm 14:1. "Miss Forehand, would you read this verse out loud?"

Audrey took the Bible from Michael and began to read. "The fool hath said in his heart, 'There is no God.' " Audrey looked at Michael in righteous indignation. "You're calling me a fool?"

"No, ma'am. God beat me to it."

The arguments continued and Audrey was brilliant with her case. But for every point, Michael countered with a Scripture. Audrey began to attend the meetings and on the last night of the meeting, Easter Sunday 1942, Audrey received Jesus as her personal Savior. Michael was thrilled with the dramatic conversion of Audrey Forehand. It had been an exciting week for the young evangelist, one that would forever change his life.

The next week, after Michael had returned home, he sent her a Bible. His desire for Audrey was that she grow in grace. Several days later he received a note thanking him for his gift.

At that time Michael was making a tour of the army camps, bringing the Good News message to the men and women of the service. Moody Bible Institute would ask Michael, "To which army camp do you feel led to go?"

Michael would reply, "The ones in Georgia!"

Moody graciously allowed him to go. On these trips, Michael made the necessary arrangements that allowed him to stop in Metter and see Audrey. Visits were brief, however, because

Michael was preaching both day and night. Before his first trip back to Metter, Michael had informed Audrey that he would be arriving about noon. But when the day came, it looked as if he might be able to surprise her with an early visit.

In those days, Metter was a town of less than three thousand people. About five miles from Audrey's home, Michael passed a farmer. They exchanged friendly waves, and Michael went on. Three miles from her home, Michael passed another farmer. Again, Michael waved to the farmer and continued on. When Michael arrived at the Forehand home, Audrey was standing out front to welcome him!

"I wanted to surprise you!" Michael said. "How did you know that I was here?"

"The farmers you waved to called me!" she explained.

Dating Audrey was like broadcasting on a party line!

In a short period of time, Michael and Audrey fell deeply in love.

Michael's mentor was evangelist Dr. W. W. Shannon. At one time, Dr. Shannon had said to Michael, "Michael, before I go home to heaven, I want to see the girl that you're going to marry! And I'd like to have a hand in picking her out!"

Later Michael told him, "I hope you like Audrey! She's the girl I'm going to marry!"

One afternoon, on his way through Metter, Dr. and Mrs. Shannon stopped at Audrey's home. "Michael will be at a week-long revival in Sebring, Florida which is where we live, and we'd like for you to consider coming down and staying in our home as a guest for the week."

"I'd like that very much."

"Wonderful! We'll drive you down!"

One evening during the revival week, Dr. Shannon asked Audrey to fry chicken. "I understand you're a wonderful cook," he coaxed.

Audrey laughed. "Yes, I suppose so!"

"Would you mind frying chicken for about thirty or forty people?"

Audrey's face registered surprise, but she quickly answered, "No. Not at all!"

Audrey went into the kitchen, which was filled with visitors, and began to prepare the chicken. Just as her hands were aptly coated in a gooey paste of flour and water, and the smell of hot grease filled the room, Michael stepped up behind her.

"Audrey, I love you. I've never said this to anyone before. . .in all of my life. . .I would like for you to be my wife."

"I love you. And I accept. But you'll have to talk to my parents."

Michael smiled. "I have! They are happily in accord! In fact, I already have your ring. You see, I don't believe in leaving anything to chance!"

Because Michael could not make it back to Georgia for a wedding, Audrey agreed to travel north for the ceremony. In November 1943 Audrey rode the train to Cleveland, Ohio, where Michael met her and rode the train back to his hometown, Lorain, Ohio, with her. As soon as they arrived, Michael stepped off the train, then turned to help Audrey down the steps. Suddenly strong arms grabbed him from behind. "You dirty rotten bluebeard! I've been chasing you through ten states! Your wives are looking for you!"

Audrey nearly fainted, but the joke was on her and Michael; the "policeman" was actually his uncle playing a practical joke on the young couple.

As soon as luggage was collected, Michael took her to his family home. Both of his parents were from Italy, so life at the Guidos' was quite different from anything Audrey had ever experienced. That night they feasted on an eight-course Italian dinner.

"What do you think of all this?" Michael asked his future bride.

"I don't know what to think! But I certainly enjoyed the meal!"

On November 25, 1943, Dr. Shannon pronounced Michael and Audrey man and wife, with Michael's superior at Moody Bible Institute serving as best man. After the wedding, the bride and groom got on a Chicago-bound train where they had a sleeper car.

"Don't go to bed until I come and have prayer with you," the best man instructed.

Audrey was obedient, in spite of Michael's insistence. "Audrey, he's not coming; he's teasing!"

But Audrey stayed up all night with her hat on, waiting for the prayer that would begin her marriage! The best man never came!

Michael couldn't have asked for a better helpmeet from the Lord! As his ministry began to grow, Audrey looked for ways to be a partner. "I can't play an instrument," she moaned. "What can I do?" Soon Audrey became one of the top female magicians in the country. . .if not the world. . .winning children to Christ with her magic act. When Michael began a radio broadcast, she learned how to be an engineer. When their ministry needed a printer for tracts, pamphlets, and so on, Audrey took on that role as well. In fact, she was so good at her job that her white printer's gloves were spotless at the end of the day. Today, Audrey continues to serve the Lord as general manager of the Guido Evangelistic Association, Inc.

Today, after more than fifty years of ministry together, Michael and Audrey's ministry releases more than thirty-five hundred radio and television broadcasts that reach the seven continents every day. Theirs was the first television ministry to release one-minute broadcasts, called "A Seed for the Garden of Your Heart," released more than one thousand times each week. Their newspaper column is printed in fifteen hundred newspapers each week, and they mail out more than one hundred thousand free daily devotional and monthly sermons for all who request them. Their ministry is home to Guido Gardens, a lush recluse of waterfalls, fountains, brooks, gazebos, topiaries, and gardens.

Michael Guido has led thousands to the Lord, but only one has he led to the altar. Without her, he says, he could have never done his life's work.

In one week, God Almighty made the universe. In one week, He built a world just for Michael Guido.

∞

*W*edding guests in Italy
throw sugared almonds at the bride and groom.

∞

*J*ohn and I had both been widowed, and when we began dating in 1983, marriage was the furthest thing from my mind. God had given me a good first marriage and I wasn't even aware that first experience could be improved upon. One Sunday after we had left church, John asked if I would like to take a motorcycle ride and I agreed. We had a delightful thirty-five-mile ride. We visited friends at the lake and just generally became better acquainted. On the way home, a deer ran out from the side of the road into our bike (which was traveling about sixty miles per hour), causing a major upset. We were both transported by ambulance to the nearest hospital where I was admitted into ICU with a concussion, multiple lacerations, and possible internal injuries. John, not having been injured seriously enough to require hospitalization, visited me regularly. After I was transferred from ICU, I asked John if he had proposed to me or if I had dreamed it. He said he had, even though if he had denied it, I wouldn't have known the difference. That was in August and we were married in November. At that time we were fifty and seventy. Now, sixteen years later, I still declare that bike accident was the best thing that ever happened to me. Otherwise, John might never have proposed! FREDA B. DOUGLAS

One Perfect Kiss

Doug and Susan Schlabach

I hear you used to attend the same church as I did in Canton." Doug Schlabach spoke quietly from one of the back pews at a small church in Dover, Ohio.

"Yes, I did," Susan Johnson answered. She had noticed Doug at her new church before, but this was the first time they had ever spoken.

"It's a large church, and I don't remember ever seeing you there. Who did you know?"

For the next few minutes, Susan shared the names of a few of the people she had known in Canton, and Doug did the same. Finally Doug said, "Would you like to join my friend and me for dinner?"

"I'd like that; yes."

That was April of 1997. From the moment of Susan's acceptance of Doug's dinner invitation until January of 1999, their relationship was a series of misunderstandings, ups and downs, and on-again, off-agains. By no means could anyone call their relationship smooth. In fact, at one point they gave up trying to make the relationship work and began to date other people. Through it

73

all Susan kept her sister's, her mother's, and her roommate Amy's ears filled with her exaltations and disappointments.

"Susan," they all advised, "make a decision, one way or the other, and stick to it."

"I can't," Susan groaned. "I just can't. This whole thing is making me crazy, and I just don't know what to do!"

Then came January of 1999 and an announcement from Doug. "Susan, I'm taking off for a weekend to fast, pray, and set some goals for this coming year," he told her over the phone. This was, ironically, during one of their off-again seasons.

"Okay," Susan answered. Other than at church, she hadn't been seeing Doug, so the call came as a surprise.

A few days later, when Doug returned, Susan was overwhelmed with the change in him. "He's more open. . .unreserved . . .straightforward. . .," Susan reported to Amy. "His eyes are different. I can see a peace that wasn't there before," she told Mary, her sister. "He seems settled, like he knows for sure what it is that he wants," she said to her mother.

"What do you think he wants?" her mother asked.

Susan grinned. "Me!"

"Has he said this?"

"Not exactly, but I can see it in his eyes. That's what is giving him away. It's like I can see into his heart."

"And what do you see?"

"The person I always knew was there, even in the midst of our struggles to communicate with each other."

Susan had seen Doug just nights before, again at church. After services, they began talking to each other inside the church. When it became late and the doors needed to be closed and locked, Susan and Doug moved to the parking lot where they sat in his truck and continued their conversation. When Susan drove home that evening, she prayed, "Lord, that's the man I want to marry. I don't know when, and I don't know how, so the rest is up to You!"

A few days later, Doug called Susan and asked her to join

him for lunch. A friend of his, Brian, joined them. When he left, Doug and Susan again moved their conversation to his truck in the parking lot.

"I want us to make a new commitment to each other," Doug began.

Susan nodded. "Okay."

"I want us to really get to know each other. To be friends. I want us to be up-front and honest in our communication. . ."

"No matter how difficult."

"No matter how difficult."

"There's something else—and this is not going to be easy, but I believe it's the best way. I just read a pamphlet called "Hold on to Your Heart," issued by Family Voice. Anyway, it has stories of couples who commit themselves to no physical touching in their courtships. No hugs. No kisses. No hand-holding."

"You're right. That won't be easy."

"No. But I think that in order to achieve our goal of true friendship and lasting commitment, we have to place the attraction and emotion between us on the back burner. It's not what's important right now."

"I agree."

She agreed then, but for the next three months, as they saw each other only in groups, Susan became increasingly frustrated with the situation.

One evening, after a late dinner after church with about twenty-five other people, Susan returned to her duplex. "I am desperately in love with Doug," Susan tearfully confided for the first time to Amy. "It's making me nuts to never have a moment alone with him and to not have his undivided attention. Doug is the one that I want! But how is this ever going to happen if we are never alone? What should I do?"

"Well, Susan! I think you've finally, truly made up your mind. You're going to marry Doug. Just wait and see!"

That night Susan fell asleep emotionally exhausted. "I know I need to be patient," she prayed before slipping between the coolness of her bed sheets. "And I know that I have to wait for Your perfect time."

In spite of her prayer the night before, the next morning Susan woke up a bit of a grouch. People at work avoided her. Midmorning, she picked up a message on her office voice mail. It was Doug. "Susan, can you meet me for lunch? Just the two of us?"

Susan's heart flipped. She immediately returned the call. "Yes, I can meet you."

"I'll pick you up at your office."

"Okay. I'll be ready."

A few hours later Susan and Doug stared at each other from across the table at Virginia's Tea Room. The air was charged with emotion as they simply gazed at each other and smiled, wordless. Eventually Susan began to speak. "Doug, I'm so frustrated by this situation we're in. Just being completely alone with you. . .is wonderful! How much longer. . .?"

The steadiness of Doug's gaze made time slow to a stop as the Italian concertina music played softly in the background. His next words rocked Susan's world. . .and changed her life forever. "I want more than anything in this world to be your husband. Will you be my wife?"

Her answer was simple. "Yes, I will!"

The newly betrothed couple smiled broadly at each other. For the first time in months, Doug reached across the table and took Susan's hand in his. Gently, ever so gently, he raised it to his lips and kissed it.

"I don't want a big wedding," Susan said, her words spilling and tumbling out.

"Me, either."

"In fact, I don't want a wedding at all!"

"We'll elope!"

"We shouldn't tell a lot of people."

True Love

"I agree!"

On the drive back to Susan's office, Doug confided, "You'll never believe this, but I didn't plan to propose to you today."

"What?!"

"I really didn't. This morning, when I was praying, I asked God to give me the right words when I talked with you today. I'll be honest with you. I was as surprised as you were when I asked! I was just speaking from my heart."

"Then I know without a doubt that this is from the Lord."

Susan's sister, Mary, was one of the few people who was told about the upcoming elopement.

"Susan, I know that the two of you want to elope. But if I'm not there to share the moment with you, I'm going to be sorely disappointed."

That settled it! Doug and Susan decided that, while they would not have a large wedding, they wouldn't elope, either. Both families were notified and invited to join them for the nuptials slated in just three weeks. In that short period of time, life was a whirlwind of activities. Because both Doug and Susan had grown up in the country, and because Doug was such an outdoorsman, Susan wanted to find the perfect location for their wedding. She chose a church in the village of Schoenbrunn, a historical site over two hundred years old and a memorial to the first settlement of Christian Indians in the state of Ohio who were converted by evangelist David Zeisburger. This lovely log church has never been updated with electricity and is lit only by candlelight. It was the perfect place for their intimate family wedding.

On June 13, 1999, in the presence of twenty-two of their immediate family members and close friends, Doug and Susan became Mr. and Mrs. Douglas Dean Schlabach.

"You may kiss your bride," the pastor said, and for the first time since their January commitment six months earlier, Doug sealed his love for Susan with a perfect kiss.

77

He has made everything beautiful in its time.
He has also set eternity in the hearts of men;
yet they cannot fathom what God has done
from beginning to end.

ECCLESIASTES 3:11 NIV

I already love your beauty, but I am only beginning to love in you that which is eternal and ever precious—your heart, your soul. Beauty one could get to know and fall in love with in one hour and cease to love it as speedily; but the soul one must learn to know. Believe me, nothing on earth is given without labour, even love, the most beautiful and natural of feelings.

COUNT LEO TOSTORI
to his fiancée, VALERIA ARSENEV

We had dated only two months when we knew. . .but I can't really say how my husband proposed. There really wasn't too much discussion. . .I think we just both knew. . . I remember telling him that he would be the perfect person for me to marry, and he said he had thought the same thing. I can't say it was love at first sight, but definitely an accelerated version of the way most relationships go!

SUE MATRAJT

Making Lemonade out of Lemons

Randell and Brendalyn Stricklin

Brendalyn Crudup sat at her desk in the accounting department of A. J. Bayless Marketing and smiled warmly at the woman who stood over her. "Brendalyn, I want you to meet my husband's cousin. He's perfect for you! His name is Randell Stricklin. He's twenty-seven years old and very nice."

Brendalyn grimaced. "Evelyn, in the past year you've introduced me to some real lemons," the nineteen-year-old said with a dry laugh. "You're one of my best friends, but your matchmaking has almost ruined our friendship on more than one occasion."

"You'll like Randell," Evelyn retorted, as if that was that. "We call him Sonny."

Later that evening Brendalyn spoke to another close friend, Erma. "The problem with Evelyn is that she thinks she's the world's greatest matchmaker."

"So are you going out with this. . .what was his name?"

"Randell. Randell Stricklin, but they call him Sonny. And to answer your question: Yeah, but I won't like it. I'm not promising to be nice, either."

Brendalyn and Sonny did meet and go out on their blind date, but they spoke on the phone a week prior. Brendalyn's lack of assurance over how well meeting and dating Sonny would go was soothed somewhat by his soft voice. However, during their first phone conversation, certain words from Sonny's mouth didn't suit Brendalyn at all!

"I just want you to know that I'm going to marry you," he said.

"Excuse me?"

"How long of a courtship do you want?"

"How long of a—"

"I realize you know very little about me. . ."

"You could say that, yes!"

". . .but that doesn't make any difference."

"On what grounds have you judged that you are going to marry me?"

"I can tell by the sound of your voice that you are the woman I've been waiting for."

"Well, I never heard of anything like this in my life!"

"You might as well get used to the fact that you will be my wife, I'd say."

When Brendalyn met the slender, broad-shouldered, handsome Sonny a week later, she didn't bother to hide her animosity. Yet, no matter how rude she was, Sonny kept calling.

"You know, Erma," she reported a few weeks later, "I think he's starting to grow on me. He really is a nice man!"

Over the next several weeks Brendalyn and Sonny enjoyed each other's company at the movies, dinners, and on sight-seeing trips to places such as the Grand Canyon.

After only three months of dating, one evening as they were watching television, Sonny turned to Brendalyn and looked her in the eyes. "Brendalyn, do you love me?"

The question wasn't unusual; he asked it almost every night. Brendalyn's typical response was, "I love you a little more than yesterday." That night, however, something in his eyes stopped her.

"Yes. I love you very much."

Sonny stood briefly then dropped to one knee. "Will you marry me?"

Brendalyn felt a bit of "brat" rising up within her and she grinned. "You'll have to call my father in Arkansas and ask permission."

Sonny took a deep breath, stood, and walked over to the

phone. "What's the number?"

Brendalyn joined him and gave him her father's phone number. Sonny dialed and waited silently for Mr. Crudup to answer. Within seconds, Brendalyn faintly heard the voice of her father. "Hello?"

"Hello, Mr. Crudup. This is Sonny Stricklin and I'm calling to ask for permission to marry your daughter."

After a moment of muffled conversation, Sonny handed the phone to Brendalyn. "He wants to talk with you."

Brendalyn took the phone. "Hey, Dad."

"Brendalyn, do you love Sonny?"

"Yes, I do."

"Then I give my blessings."

Brendalyn looked up at Sonny and smiled. "Dad says that I can marry you."

Five months later Brendalyn married the young man she had not been so kind to. "If I could go back and change anything," she told Erma some time later, "I would have been nicer when I first met Sonny. Who knew?"

Erma laughed. "I'd have to say Evelyn! Looks like you took her lemon and made lemonade!"

The wedding cake was originally called bride cake. In the day of the Romans, it was made with grain and salt, and in Greece it was made with pounded grain and honey. In Denmark the traditional wedding cake is the cornucopia cake, which is filled with candy, almond cakes, and fresh fruit. The wedding cake has been an iced marzipan cake, a fruitcake, and the traditional white cake. After the Civil War, the custom of a dark cake for the groom's cake and a white cake for the bride's cake began.

The Heartwarmer

Rev. Tom and Pat Lacy

How would you like to become Mrs. Mini-Storage?" The sound of rumbling thunder blended with the pelting downpour of rain on the automobile roof of Tom's car as he and Pat McDaniel headed toward Pat's townhouse, nearly drowning out the question.

Tom Lacy, manager of Staples Mill Mini-Storage, was very serious. His date, Pat, was floored. After all, it was only their first official date, March 17, 1983—St. Patrick's Day—a dark and stormy night.

Their story actually began on a brighter day, three years earlier. In September 1980 Tom had begun attending a church where Pat had been a member since 1976. Grove Avenue Baptist Church of Richmond, Virginia, had a friendly, growing singles' ministry. Visitors were warmly welcomed and urged to participate in the many activities. The members of the singles' ministry were a tight bunch. They sat together in church, went out to eat after services, and got together every time an opportunity arose. Because Tom managed Staples Mill Mini-Storage, the group had a readymade parking lot, making Tom a fairly popular member of the group.

"Tom, would you consider teaching a Sunday school class?" Rev. Guy Holloway, the pastor of the singles' ministry, asked. Tom had been attending the church only a short period of time and he was thrilled at the request.

"Absolutely," Tom answered.

Nearly twenty people signed up for the class, including Patricia McDaniel. A few weeks into his new duties as teacher, Tom received a phone call from Pat.

"I have two prayer requests," she told him. "I am working three part-time jobs right now. It's the desire of my heart to work only one—and that it be enough to support me."

"Sure thing, Pat. And your next one?"

"An unspoken request."

Tom was aware of a Christian couple who was in need of a full-time secretary. A few phone calls and an interview later, Pat had the job. Six weeks later, however, Pat was rushed to the hospital because of a gallbladder attack. Once she was settled in her room, she called her employer. "I have to have surgery in the morning," Pat informed them. The sound of her voice was evidence of the pain that racked her body.

"I'm sorry, Pat," she was told, "we can't hold your job for you."

Pat was stunned. "Then may I ask if you put me on your hospitalization policy?"

"No. We never got around to doing that."

Pat hung up the phone in disbelief, then called the insurance company to see if she was covered. Within moments after ending that phone call, she dialed Tom's number.

"I'm in the hospital, Tom. I have to have gallbladder surgery in the morning. My parents can't get here—the snowstorm, you know. My insurance is in force, but a payment has to be made before midnight tonight. I know it's cold out—and snowing—but could you possibly make the payment for me?"

"Not a problem, Pat. I'll be up at the hospital in just a bit for your check. I'll be more than happy to take care of this for you."

There was a pause before Pat returned, "By the way, how do you know God's will for your life?"

"We'll do some Bible study when I come to pick up your check."

When Tom arrived at Pat's hospital room, he answered Pat's question, using marriage as an illustration. "It's God who is in the heartwarming business, Pat. Not man. For example, it's not up to me to sweep some gal off her feet. God warms a heart or two. Then the two pursue the relationship if they so choose. God's will is not measured by whom you marry, but God is most definitely concerned about whom you marry."

Tom could tell that Pat didn't like the illustration, even though he certainly was neither hinting at anything between them nor knowingly "seed planting" for future harvest. Nor could he have known then that at one time Pat's heart had been warm for a young man while the two of them were in high school. When he went to college, he mailed the infamous "Dear Jane" letter. Pat had kept her heart closely guarded ever since.

Yet before her stood a man who was willing to drive out in the cold and the snow, to make an insurance payment for her, and to gently illustrate God's will for her life.

Pat's surgery went well. Her parents arrived before she was released from the hospital. As soon as she was up to it, Tom became a regular visitor. Mr. and Mrs. McDaniel were charmed by Tom, but Pat clearly wasn't. Soon, Pat was back into the swing of things and her relationship with Tom returned to normal.

One Sunday evening after services, Tom surprised himself when he confided to Pat, "You know, you are getting to be kinda special to me."

"Yeah, me too," Pat replied, a shock to them both.

Tom was correct about God being in the heartwarming business. He could neither deny his feelings for Pat nor delay his desire to take her out. When he asked her out for St. Patrick's Day, he was pleased when she said yes, but he shocked even himself when he blurted out, "How would you like to be Mrs. Mini-Storage?"

Pat, taken aback, smiled but did not answer.

The following Sunday, while eating lunch with the singles' group, Tom leaned over and said, "I don't mind waiting forever, Pat. As long as forever doesn't take forever."

Pat smiled. Perhaps she was ready to give her heart away again.

September 3, 1983, Pat joined her heart to Tom's, but not before filling him in on a little secret. "Remember our first date? I only went out with you to tell you that I wasn't interested in you. Then, as I remember, I came completely unglued the night that you used marriage as an illustration. What was that about?"

"It wasn't meant to be anything more than teaching. I suppose it came to me because as members of the singles' group, we spend so much time talking about dating and marriage."

Pat nodded. "It was probably the Holy Spirit planting a seed. Otherwise, why would I have gotten so upset by the suggestion?"

Yes, that settles it. Only God can truly warm a heart.

We're too old to be single. Why shouldn't we both be married instead of sitting through the long winter evenings by our solitary firesides? Why shouldn't we make one fireside of it?

Come, let's be a comfortable couple and take care of each other! How glad we shall be, that we have somebody we are fond of always, to talk to and sit with.

Let's be a comfortable couple. Now do, my dear!

CHARLES DICKENS

$\mathcal{J}$ was working forty hours a week and going to college about forty hours a week. My life was a little crazy, so I made a decision not to date until I had graduated. Not more than a week had gone by when I had my first date with Dawn. I didn't really plan for it to build to anything— I thought she was interested in one of my roommates—so I don't really know what I was thinking. By the third or fourth date, I was pretty well blown away by her! Two months later I took her out for a Mexican dinner and then to the beach. I parked the car and we began to walk away from the crowd. We sat on the sand and began to talk. She more or less thought we were going to do devotions on the beach; I read some special verses to her, then stood and told her to get up. She didn't want to, really, so I kinda pulled her up and walked her down to the water's edge. I knelt down and washed her feet, then told her that I wanted to serve the Lord forever and that I wanted to serve Him with her.

She began to tear up and she said, "Okay."

I reached into my pocket and, still kneeling before her, extended the ring and asked, "Will you marry me?"

She said, "Yes." I stood up and we hugged each other in ankle-deep water.

CHRIS RUSSELL

$\mathcal{J}$t took great courage to ask
a beautiful young woman to marry me.
Believe me, it is easier to play
the whole of *Petrushka* on the piano.

ARTUR RUBINSTEIN,
Concert Pianist

Chance Meeting

David and Carmen Leal Pock

Carmen Leal sat in the social hall of Parents Without Partners and fumed. She didn't want to be there. She had just returned to her home in Hawaii from a business trip in Nashville and she was tired. Had it not been for the whining of her friend, Bonnie, she'd be in the quiet solitude of her home.

Quiet it would have been, too. Her two sons, Nicholas, age seven, and Justin, age six, were on the mainland with her sister. So right now. . .this very second. . .she'd be home and not at this informational meeting of Parents Without Partners. She didn't need to be there anyway, she told herself. She was already a member. It was Bonnie who needed to be there. . .

Carmen scanned the room for her friend one more time and scowled. It was Bonnie who had so adamantly wanted to be there tonight. So where was she? Carmen began to move through the room and reminded herself of why she had joined PWP in the first place.

Joining PWP hadn't been a move to find a man. Even though tight finances were sometimes an issue, Carmen was content with her single status. She owned her own business and her home, was active in her music and speaking ministry, and attended a supportive and wonderful church filled with friends. But she was concerned that her sons needed proper male role models. Their father, who worked nights and weekends, wasn't a Christian, and PWP gave Nicholas and Justin the opportunity for positive family activities such as camping, bowling, and the movies.

"Where is she?" Carmen asked out loud this time. The room was filling. More people. . .no Bonnie.

"Hey, let's get started, shall we?" A voice brought the room to attention. Carmen fumed; the meeting was beginning and her friend still had not shown. Her dark brown eyes scanned the room in a final effort and locked with those of a tall man standing at the top of the steps. He looked lost, and in the state Carmen was in, she quickly broke the contact and moved to a chair, hoping that he wouldn't sit next to her. The last thing she needed this evening was a single father looking for a single mother.

Sure enough, he came down the steps, strolled across the room, and sat next to her.

As the group began by introducing themselves to those around them, Carmen heard the tall man introduce himself as David and say that he was from Phoenix.

"No, you're not," she said harshly. "You're from Oklahoma or something."

"How did you know that? I'm from Oklahoma City, but I've lived in Phoenix almost twenty years."

"You look like a farmer. Are you German?"

"Yes! How did you know that?"

"You look like my ex-in-laws. Are you a Nazi? My ex was a German and he was a Nazi." Inwardly Carmen scolded herself for being so cruel, but outwardly she couldn't seem to stop herself.

"No!" he exclaimed. "I'm really nice! Would it help if I told you I was part Irish?"

"Oh, great! A drunk Nazi!"

The tone for the meeting was pretty much set with Carmen being downright rude. She couldn't explain herself—even to herself! Why was she being so hateful to this perfectly nice man?

By eight o'clock the meeting was over and Carmen was feeling awful about her behavior. She decided to apologize to the tall man with the kind brown eyes.

"I just wanted to apologize for the way I acted this evening. I was supposed to meet my friend Bonnie here and she stood me up. I didn't even want to be here. . .my kids are on the mainland with my sister and I had hoped for a quiet evening at home."

"That's okay."

"When did you move to Hawaii?"

"Just recently. My two kids are back in Phoenix and I'm here on a job search."

"I'm pretty well-connected on the island," Carmen began as she fished a business card from her purse. "Call me if you need any help."

David took the card and nodded. "I understand some of the group is going dancing. Do you want to go?"

"Not really, no. I have no rhythm so I don't dance. But this month when we have our karaoke night, I'll be there."

"What's that?"

Carmen explained the entertainment that had originated in Japan. "A screen displays the words to songs while the music plays. Hear it, see it, sing it. It's really a lot of fun."

"It's pretty early still. Would you take me to one?"

Carmen figured it was the least she could do. "Sure. I can do that. There's one not too far from here."

David drove his car and followed Carmen's to the Karaoke Club at the Holiday Inn. Once inside, Carmen said, "Choose a couple of songs for me to sing."

"Okay. Sing 'Close To You.' "

Having sung the popular hit countless times at weddings, Carmen had promised herself that she would never sing it again. Yet, there she stood singing the popular tune to a man who was quickly—and obviously—falling in love with her.

Carmen was disgusted!

After a few more songs and a little conversation, Carmen announced that she needed to get home.

"So soon?"

"I'm singing at church tomorrow, so I really should get some sleep."

"Where do you go to church?"

"Faith Baptist Church in Kailua."

"I'll be there!"

Carmen forced a smile. Great.

The next morning when David walked into the sanctuary for services, Carmen was not happy. She decided that she would somehow, some way, get rid of him as soon as the services were over.

"I have to hurry home to make something for a going-away party this afternoon," she explained later.

"I'll help."

"Well, then I have to go to the party, so—"

"I'll go with you!"

That afternoon, whether she liked it or not, David was Carmen's shadow. That evening, when they heard a commercial for a movie, David said, "We should take your kids to see that movie when they come back from your sister's."

This was where she was putting her foot down. "Sorry, but my kids don't meet strange men. They will only meet the man I'm going to marry."

David never batted an eyelash. "Yeah, I know. So when do they come home so I can meet them?"

Carmen decided that the man was just plain dense.

"Now about tomorrow. . .would you like to go out with me?"

"I'm volunteering at the homeless shelter."

"Great! I used to do that in Phoenix! I'll come with you."

And so it was that their second date was a trip to a homeless shelter.

Their third date was a Bible study that Carmen attended, and their fourth date was a Bible study that she was leading. At times Carmen felt that David was no more than a tagalong, but. . .she had to admit. . .he was growing on her.

On Thursday he called Carmen to ask her out for another date.

"David, you have monopolized all my time. I have paperwork

to do and a house to clean. You will have to stay away from me!"

"How about if I clean your house? Would you then have time to do your paperwork?"

"I suppose. . ."

"Then I can take you out to dinner."

"Okay. Sure."

An hour later David arrived at Carmen's home with cleaning supplies and plastic gloves. As Carmen tackled the growing stack of papers on her desk, David scrubbed her toilet.

"This I could get used to," she said to herself with a chuckle.

When they were both done with their respective jobs, Carmen announced, "I feel bad that you've had to work so hard around here. Why don't I cook you dinner rather than you taking me out?"

"Works for me."

The evening—the entire day—would have been perfect had it not been for one thing: David's constant chatter about marriage.

Three days later, just eight days after having met for the first time, David sat on the beach and listened to Carmen sing at the "Church on the Beach" sponsored by the Waikiki Beach Chaplaincy.

"I have to pick my kids up tomorrow at the airport," Carmen announced later.

"Good. I want to meet them."

Carmen knew that by saying yes to David going with her, she was, in reality, saying yes to a marriage proposal. She drew a deep breath and met him squarely in the eyes. "Okay," she said.

They both understood what the "okay" meant, and not long after David met her kids, he became her husband.

Two are better than one,
because they have a good return for their work:
If one falls down,
his friend can help him up.

ECCLESIASTES 4:9–10 NIV

Slippery Excuse

Hal and Marie Asher

Marie Black answered her telephone on the third ring. "Marie, this is Marge."

"Oh, hi, Marge. What's up?"

"So glad you asked! There's a guy I want you to meet. He's new in town—was transferred here, to St. Paul, about two months ago—and I think you two would really hit it off. He's very nice, but he seems so lonely and I was thinking that perhaps you could befriend him. . .introduce him to some people more his age."

Marie smiled at the words of her mother's friend, Marge. Dear, kind, sweet Marge, who thought that Marie, at twenty-five, was an old maid and in need of some matchmaking. "Oh, Marge."

"His name is Hal," Marge continued. "He's very nice."

"You said that," Marie replied with a chuckle.

"I know that you usually say 'no' to my fixing you up, so this time I gave him your phone number."

"Oh, Marge!" In spite of the situation, she laughed.

Two nights later, Hal Asher called Marie. Marge was right;

Hal was nice and the conversation flowed easily. By the end of the half-hour conversation, Marie asked Hal to join her at an upcoming Christmas party. "I teach music at Brookside Elementary School. We're having a Christmas party on Friday. Would you like to go with me?" Marie's thoughts were twofold. Hal did seem like a nice man, and she wanted to meet him. Taking him to the Christmas party would put them in a safe, public place.

"Sounds good," Hal said.

Marie was impressed with Hal from the beginning. When he came to pick her up for the party and they were heading out the door, he helped her with her coat. Upon reaching his car, he opened her car door. Furthermore, to Marie's delight, Hal fit right in with her coworkers. Before the night was over, Hal invited Marie to go with him to a movie on Sunday and she accepted.

Saturday night, St. Paul was blanketed in snow, so on Sunday Hal and Marie felt it was best not to drive to the theater.

"There is a restaurant a few blocks from here," Marie said. "If you'd like, we can just go down there for something to eat. . . get some hot coffee. . .talk. . ."

Hal readily agreed. During the dinner Marie began to agree with Marge; Hal was lonely. She invited Hal to Christmas dinner at her mother's house. "She lives about sixty miles from here in Millsburg. I think you'd have a good time. My father died a few years ago, so it's just Mom and me."

"Marie, I have to tell you that I'm Jewish."

Marie was quiet, but for only a moment. "That's okay. You can still come and have dinner with us."

"I'm going to be up that way on business, staying at a motel there, so sure, I'd love to."

Two weeks later, Hal joined Marie and her family for Christmas dinner. When he arrived at her mother's home, his arms were filled with gifts. Marie's gift was a bottle of perfume.

Perfume? This is going too fast, Marie thought. But she truly liked him.

Two days later, while still in Millsburg, Hal and Marie went to a movie. Afterward, when they were settled in Hal's car, Marie suggested something totally on impulse. "There's a park that overlooks the river. Want to go there?"

Hal laughed, realizing that this was a place for young lovers to go, then started his car and headed in the direction Marie gave him. It wasn't too long into the park, however, before Marie was looking out the window at the piles of snow, thinking, *Not such a good idea.*

No sooner had she thought it than the wheels of Hal's car were stuck in the snow. With an exasperated sigh, Hal opened the car door and stepped out. "Let me see what I can do." And then he promptly slipped and fell, knocking himself unconscious.

"Hal!" Marie exclaimed as she carefully made her way out and around the car to Hal's limp form. "Hal! Come to! Come to! Hal Asher, you're too heavy for me to pick up and carry to the hospital! Hal!"

Moments later a groggy Hal managed to pull himself up. "If you steer, I'll push the car out of this rut," Hal instructed.

"Are you sure?"

"Yeah. I'll push. You steer."

A short time later, Hal and Marie trudged their way to a nearby house where they stopped and asked if they could come inside to use the phone. While Hal took a seat to rest, Marie called for a tow truck and then her mother. "Might as well," she mumbled to herself. "Tow truck driver's mother is a friend of Mom's, so she's going to find out anyway."

When Marie returned to Hal, she reported, "Tow truck is on its way. So is my mother."

"Your mother?"

Marie nodded sheepishly.

"She's going to know that we were going to go park by the

river, isn't she?" Hal asked.

Marie smiled, then nodded again.

The tow truck and Marie's mother arrived shortly thereafter. "Mrs. Black," Hal quickly began, "I would never have taken your daughter to such a place if I didn't have the intention of asking her to marry me."

"What!" Marie exclaimed. "Marry you?"

"Will you?"

Without so much as a pause, Marie answered, "Let me think about it."

Hal blushed and Marie continued. "I want to make sure you're fully conscious!"

Eventually, Marie accepted. Because of the difference in their religious background, Hal tried to find a rabbi to marry them in a private ceremony that would be followed by a large reception. There were three rabbis in town. Two were on vacation and the other one would not marry them without the consent of the other two. Finally, Marie's pastor said that he would marry them privately, as they wished.

But friends and family had a different idea. When word "got out" that "the old maid" was getting married, a large wedding with three hundred guests resulted. No regrets. Hal Asher and Marie Black became man and wife in a traditional Christian wedding on July 10, 1968. Over thirty years have passed and Hal continues to claim that when he asked Marie to marry him, he was under the effects of a concussion.

Blessed art Thou, O Lord our God, King of the universe, who hath created joy and sadness, bridegroom and bride, mirth, exultation, pleasure and delight, love and brotherhood, and peace and friendship. O Lord our God, may there soon be heard in the cities of Judah and in the streets of Jerusalem the voice of joy and the voice of gladness, the voice of the bridegroom and the voice of the bride, the jubilant voice of the bridegrooms from their canopies and of youths from their feasts of song. Blessed are Thou, O Lord, who maketh the bridegroom to rejoice with the bride.   JEWISH PRAYER

In the heavens he has pitched a tent for the sun,
which is like a bridegroom coming forth
from his pavilion,
like a champion rejoicing to run his course.

PSALM 19:4–5 NIV

It had been a fun evening out dancing with Dad, my boyfriend, Ed, my sister and her husband. When our legs could no longer carry us along the dance floor, we called it a night. Ed and I decided to go for a ride. We found a quiet spot under a chestnut tree in the parking lot of the Greek Church across the street from Nana's house. We were sharing our thoughts as dating couples do. Ed paused for a moment and finally was able to say, "A penny for your thoughts."

I wasn't quite sure what to say, so I countered with, "A penny for yours."

He came back eventually with, "Will you marry me?"

Of course, I said, "Yes." This was the boy who held my high school books for me as we walked through the halls at school! We've been married for thirty-five years now. A well-spent penny can take a person a very long way!

KAREN HANSON

⚭

The highest love of all finds
its fulfillment not in what it keeps,
but in what it gives.

FR. ANDREW SCD,
Seven Words from the Cross

⚭

A Groovy Kind of Love

Mike and Deneene Winters

On a warm August evening in 1980, at Western Pancake House in Parkersburg, West Virginia, seventeen-year-old Deneene Marie Artherhults was working the first shift of her new job.

"You've got customers at table seven, Deneene," a coworker informed her. "They just sat down."

Deneene smiled warmly as she grabbed a tray and filled it

with water glasses. As she approached the table where several young men sat, she heard one of the "older" men say to one of the "younger" men, "Hey, Barry, check out the new waitress! She sure is good-looking." The man speaking was Mike Winters. Deneene instantly noted his good looks and deep dimples, but she was naïve and not quite prepared for what would happen next.

"Hi, doll," Barry said, looking directly at Deneene. "What are you doing for the rest of your life?"

"I've got plans," Deneene retorted, then whirled around and walked away. The men roared with laughter.

"She's not that good-looking," Barry came back.

"I think she's even better-looking now," Mike returned.

"Yeah, yeah," Barry said. "If you think you're all that good, Mike, why don't you try your luck?"

"What? That little girl is way too young for me."

Deneene stopped short, turned around, and walked back to the table. "No, I'm not."

"Well, then. What are you doing tomorrow?"

Dating for Deneene and Mike usually meant movies, playing pool, or a trip to the mall. On one of their shopping excursions Mike pulled a pair of Calvin Klein jeans from a rack.

"Try these on. If they fit, I'll buy them for you," he told her.

"These jeans?"

"They're Calvin Klein's."

"Who's that?"

The handsome man in front of her laughed.

"He's a designer. Now go try them on."

Deneene obeyed. The jeans fit beautifully, something Mike noted as soon as she stepped out of the dressing room. "You look good in those jeans. I'm buying them for you."

Deneene grabbed for the price tag. Seeing the exorbitance of it, she balked. "Mike, no! They're too expensive!"

Mike playfully placed his hands firmly on the young girl's shoulders and spun her around. "Go take them off so I can buy them for you."

"Mike! I just can't let you!"

"Tell you what, you can pay the tax."

Deneene and Mike dated for the next two weeks, until it was time for the twenty-three-year-old business major to return to Kentucky where he was attending Eastern Kentucky University. Deneene returned to Parkersburg High School for her senior year of high school. Whenever the opportunity to return to Parkersburg arose, Mike would hitchhike the 310 miles home to see Deneene. During the weekend of January 17, 1981, as a thick veil of snow fell from the West Virginia skies, Deneene didn't expect to see her boyfriend of five months walk through the front door of her home. Then came an unexpected knock.

"Mike!" Deneene exclaimed, throwing her arms around the man she had come to love.

"What do you want to do tonight?" he asked her.

"I don't care. Let's just go to the mall and walk around." They did just that.

Later Mike asked, "What do you want to do next?"

"Do you want to go to City Park?"

"Sure."

"Or we can go get some ice cream!"

"Okay. We can do both!"

"Okay." Mike groaned slightly. "I thought you'd turn me down on doing both."

"You're stuck now, mister."

Mike drove to the home of his parents in nearby Vienna, West Virginia, and retrieved a couple of spoons, then to Kroger's Grocery Store where he and Deneene purchased a pint of strawberry shortcake ice cream. Minutes later they drove to City Park where Mike parked next to an isolated picnic table close to the city's still-lit Christmas tree.

"I'm going to leave the radio on so we can listen to the music," Mike said. He and Deneene got out and walked over to the table. "Let me wipe the snow off here," Mike said as he handed the ice cream to Deneene. "Hold this." In the glow of the tree lights, Mike and Deneene laughed and shivered as they spooned the ice cream. "This is fun," Mike said.

Deneene placed another spoonful of ice cream into her mouth. "This is good!" They laughed again.

"I want you to marry me." The unexpected words hung in the frosty air.

"I want to marry you!" Deneene exclaimed. Just that easy—just that quick.

Mike whooped as Deneene squealed in delight. They jumped off the table, hugged, and began to dance in the snow to the tunes that came from the car's radio.

For the next fifteen months, Mike and Deneene endured the pessimistic opinions of family and friends. "It will never last," they said. "Deneene is too young."

In spite of that, they spoke vows of eternal commitment on April 3, 1982, in the living room of Mike's parents and in the presence of their families and friends. Some relationships are meant to last forever. The year 2000 brought with it the eighteenth anniversary of the wedding of Mike and Deneene Winters. "Baby, you and me, we've got a groovy kind of love," Mike sang as the big day approached. Their unlikely success story has included three children, Donovan, Cassie, and Krischan, and a lifetime of activity in their community, in the preservation of the environment, and within the body of their church. Their household includes five human members and enough animals to start their own zoo. Typical days are filled with work, school, dance and music, reading and painting, and enough love to last a lifetime. They've got a groovy kind of love.

A solemn thing it was, I said
A woman white to be,
And wear, if God should count me fit,
Her hallowed mystery.

A timid thing to drop a life
Into the purple well,
Too plummetless that it comes back
Eternity until.

EMILY DICKINSON
"Wedded"

Life Preserver

Cliff and La Marilys Doering

*C*an you sew?" Cliff Doering asked his girlfriend of six months, La Marilys Wheaton.

"Yes, I can sew. Why?"

"Can you make a Hawaiian shirt for me and a muumuu for you?"

La Marilys laughed. "For what?"

"National Management Association is having a steak fry/luau. And listen to this: One of the special interludes of this dinner dance is a cruise on San Diego Bay."

"It sounds wonderful."

And it was. On a warm August evening, with a full moon hanging in the black sky over the bay, Cliff and La Marilys climbed the steps to the upper deck of the cruise ship as a golden oldies band played.

"Let's have a seat over here," Cliff suggested as he indicated a couple of deck chairs near them. After they sat and had deeply breathed in the night air, Cliff noted, "Look at that moon."

"It's incredible."

"This is one of the most beautiful places to be—day or night."

"But especially tonight," La Marilys commented. "Look. The moon is dancing on the water."

"So are the lights from the city. There's not a ripple on the water."

La Marilys was quiet for a moment, then softly added, "Dinner was good."

"Dinner was great!"

"Did you enjoy the music and dancing?"

La Marilys turned to Cliff and smiled. "You are a very romantic man, Mr. Doering. Yes, I enjoyed it very much. Thank you for asking me to join you this evening."

The sounds of the band playing "Moonlight Bay" drifted up the stairs to where Cliff and La Marilys sat. Cliff reached into his pocket, brought out a small box, and handed it to La Marilys. "You may want to open this because it's your life preserver in case the boat sinks."

La Marilys noted the twinkle in his eyes and she furrowed her brow. "Those are strange words considering that we're on a smooth cruise in the middle of a calm bay." But curiosity aroused, she opened the box. Inside was a lovely engagement ring.

Cliff continued. "This is to assure preservation for the rest of your life. Will you say yes?"

Somewhere in the middle of laughter, tears, and hugs, La Marilys said, "Yes!"

Later they went below. Word soon spread that the happy couple was engaged. The entertainers, a barbershop quartet, serenaded them. Two months later, they gifted them by entertaining the wedding guests.

On October 21, 1972, Cliff and La Marilys began sailing toward a wonderful life of caring, adventure, joy, and love as they docked in and out of many trying circumstances. At one point in their marriage they owned and operated their own business. In doing so they began spending twenty-four hours a day together.

"How can you do that?" a friend asked incredulously.

Cliff's immediate response followed. "We got married to be together. We thank God every day for bringing us together. . . for teaching us to love Him. . .and for His Son Who has first place in our home."

There is no fear in love.
But perfect love drives out fear. . . .

1 JOHN 4:18 NIV

A Special Date

Scott and Stephanie Townley

With career primarily on her mind, Stephanie Tashiro promised God and her parents that she would not date until she was twenty-five. In April of 1992, just one month before her twenty-fifth birthday, Stephanie, a clarinet teacher at a music shop in Kirkland, Washington, stopped by the shop to check in with the owner. After talking about various business-related things, Rick commented, "There is a wedding band I know of that is looking for a singer."

"You're kidding! I just came back from a studio where one of my best friends is a recording engineer. We recorded a tape of me singing a cappella. I want to find a band that could back me up at weddings and things like that."

"Give it to me. I can listen to it with another one of the band members. Would you like to come on my boat with me tomorrow?"

Stephanie shook her head. "No, thank you. But I appreciate your passing this on for me," she continued as she handed the tape to Rick.

The next day, Scott Townley heard the tape. "Wow!" he exclaimed. "Her voice is great! I love it! What is she like as a person?"

Rick said, "She is a very spiritual person and very professional."

Scott replied, "I can't wait to meet her."

After a few phone conversations and a number of weeks passed, Stephanie went to her first evening rehearsal. There she met with Rick (the bassist), Scott (the pianist), and Loren (the saxophonist). Scott instantly became a friend.

"Hey, Scott," Stephanie greeted him one evening. "I'm having a birthday party next week, on the sixteenth. Would you like to come?"

"Oh, Stephanie, I would love to come, but I'll be out of town. Sorry."

Stephanie smiled in return. "That's okay. But if your plans change. . ."

"Thanks. I'll keep that in mind."

Scott didn't make it to Stephanie's party, but the following day at rehearsal, he presented her with a tambourine. "Happy birthday, Stephanie," he said.

"Scott! Thank you! That's so sweet!" Stephanie said while thinking, *Does he think I'm like someone from the cartoon Josie and the Pussycats?* Stephanie dismissed this thought as she remembered that it was the thought that counted.

After rehearsal Scott and Stephanie walked out and talked about the party and other band-related things as they strolled over to his car as usual.

"How do you like singing with the band so far?"

"I like it a lot, but I'd like to see us do more jazz. I love jazz. And maybe some more love songs from movies. You know, that kind of thing."

"Sounds good to me. We should start working on that."

Moments of silence passed before Stephanie and Scott continued in the conversation, which was light and full of fun and banter. When they reached Stephanie's car, Scott asked a question he had been thinking about for weeks.

"Stephanie? May I give you a kiss?"

Stephanie smiled. "Yes." A kiss later, she added, "Do you mind if I ask what your intentions are in this relationship?"

"To marry you, when you are ready and know that you love me, too."

Their dating period officially began.

Two weeks later Scott came to downtown Seattle where Stephanie worked full time. "Because you're only picking me up to drive me home, if you want short-term free parking, park at the apartment complex right around the corner," Stephanie told Scott over the telephone. "The manager knows me well and you'll only be here long enough to walk to my office building, so I'm sure it will be okay."

"That'll work."

But Scott arrived earlier than expected, which meant he parked in the "potential new resident parking area" longer than expected.

"I feel bad that you were there so long," Stephanie said. "I know. Since I know the manager, why don't you go in and look at the facilities, too, and I can introduce you to her. That way we can park here."

Minutes later, the manager of the complex was showing Scott and Stephanie the facilities. Upon arriving at the recreation facilities, Stephanie told the apartment manager, "I don't want to take up any more of your time. Why don't you go back to work and I'll show Scott the rest of the facility."

After a few minutes of looking at pool tables, the swimming pool, and the clubhouse, Scott suddenly declared, "Hey, we could move in here!"

"No, no. Remember that we are not living together before marriage. And I know you don't plan to ask me to marry you today. We've only known each other for two months!"

"Will you marry me?"

Stephanie stammered out a stunned, "Yeah. Sure. Okay."

With an elated shout, Scott said, "Oh, yeeeessss! Let's go to the Spaghetti Factory to celebrate!"

It was three months later before Scott and Stephanie set their wedding date for May 29, 1993. Months went by as the couple prepared for their wedding. Then, one day in March of 1993, Scott showed Stephanie something startling.

"It's my letter of confirmation in the Lutheran church," he said. "Look at the date."

" 'May 29, 1977,' " Stephanie read. "The same date as our wedding. . .only sixteen years later! Hmmm."

"What?"

"Hold on a sec," Stephanie said, then headed down the hall toward her bedroom. When she returned, she held her Bible in her hand. "Scott, look. This is the Bible I received the day I asked the Lord into my heart. Look at the date written inside."

Scott took the Bible and opened to the first page. "Presented to Stephanie Tashiro, May 29, 1977." Scott looked up at his fiancée in surprise. "The same date!"

Stephanie's eyes brimmed with tears as she slid her arms around Scott's neck. "No matter what challenges we encounter," she whispered, "we must remember, the Lord showed us this to remind us that He brought us together."

Scott nodded in agreement. "I knew the moment I heard your voice that I wanted to marry you. I had been working up my nerve to ask you out since I heard the tape. The night I gave you the tambourine I took a chance. Did I ever tell you that?"

Stephanie shook her head, no.

"I love you, Stephanie."

Stephanie gave a gentle squeeze. "I love you, too."

- Armenian weddings include the releasing of two white doves, symbolizing love and happiness.

- Japanese brides and their families visit the groom's home on the day of the wedding.

- Korean weddings include ducks. Ducks mate for life.

- In Vietnam, the groom's mother visits the home of the bride and delivers a plant and pink chalk. The plant is to pay respect, the chalk represents her wish for a rosy future.

Let all thy joys be as the month of May,
And all thy days be as a marriage day:
Let sorrow, sickness, and a troubled mind
Be stranger to thee.

FRANCIS QUARLES
"To a Bride"

∞

Dear Old Golden Rule Days

Orris and Barbara Anson

Hey, Barbara!" Sixteen-year-old Orris Anson fell into step with his classmate from Fullerton Union High School in Fullerton, California, as she was walking home from school. The year was 1956.

Barbara Barrington turned to the young man she had gone to school with since fifth grade but hardly knew. "Hi, Orris."

"Walking home from school?"

"That's right."

"Mind if I walk with you?"

A cool January breeze blew through Barbara's long blond hair. "No, I don't mind."

Momentary silence began to march with them until young Orris drew in a breath and with a sigh announced, "There's a basketball game on Friday. Would you like to go with me?"

Barbara smiled. "Sure. That'd be fun!"

Orris nodded. "It's a date, then."

When Barbara arrived home, she immediately called some

of her girlfriends. "What do you know about Orris Anson?" she asked. "I know we've been going to school together all these years, but I really don't know a lot about him."

"He's a football star," one reported.

"He's a track star," another said.

"Aren't you both involved in student government?" asked still another.

"Yes, I believe we are. I take a few college prep classes with him as well."

"Why do you ask, Barbara?"

"He asked me to go to the game with him on Friday."

"Are you going?"

"I told him I would. . ."

With that, as winter became spring, young love began to blossom. For the next twenty months, Orris and Barbara dated exclusively. They were a part of a large circle of friends. Orris continued in sports while Barbara was active on the drill team. Most of their dates centered around school activities, studying together, miniature golf, movies, drives to the mountains or the beach, driving along the ocean in Orris's red MG with the top down. Sunday mornings were spent in church. One special outing was to the Christmas Eve service at Orris's church. It was their senior year of high school.

The following summer, on a hot August afternoon, Orris left Fullerton for Colorado School of Mines in Colorado. Barbara remained in California where she attended the University of Redlands. She would eventually graduate from the University of Southern California. It was during this time period, in these places, that young love was tested.

Orris and Barbara were in love, and they wanted to get married eventually, but obtaining their college degrees was important to both of them. It seemed the right thing to do—finish school and then marry. But Colorado and California seemed lifetimes away for Orris and Barbara. Correspondence, no matter how frequent, was a poor substitute for being together. Eventually, there were the misunderstandings. . . .

It was during their freshman years at college that Barbara received a letter from Orris. As she read it, her face fell.

"What's wrong?" her roommate asked.

"Orris doesn't want to see me anymore."

"He wrote that in the letter?"

"He didn't say it exactly. . .but in so many words, that's what he's saying!"

"You should write him back. . ."

"No! I won't give him the satisfaction!"

At the end of his first semester, Orris returned to Fullerton to attend Fullerton Junior College. With the content of the letter between them, Christmas 1957 was much different than it had been the year before. On Valentine's Day 1958, Barbara received a box of delicious See's Chocolates from Orris. As she savored each delectable bite, she shook her head at her frowning roommate. "Won't do him a bit of good!" she exclaimed. "Want a chocolate?"

Sometime later, Barbara ran into a former high school classmate. "I guess you know that Orris is dating someone at Fullerton. . . ."

Barbara was crushed. "No, I didn't know. . ."

"A cute little blond he met there. I don't know her name. . ."

Later Barbara cried to her roommate. "I can't believe it! He's seeing someone else! A cute little blond!"

"I thought you didn't want him!" the roommate exclaimed.

"I'm miffed at him, but he's still first in my heart and I still want to be first in his heart!"

Soon after, Orris was approached by another mutual friend. "I hear Barbara is dating someone from Redlands. Man, what happened to you two?"

"I don't have the foggiest idea. I must have done something

or said something. . .I honestly don't know! Well, that settles it. There's no point in continuing this and I might as well give up. Time to get on with life."

Indeed, for the next three decades, life went on. . .

In mid-July 1991, Orris sat down at his kitchen table with pad and pen and wrote a letter to Barbara.

> *Dear Barbara,*
> *I don't know if this letter will reach you or not. I found your address in our class reunion booklet. I'm aware of the possibility that it may not be correct. I have moved nine times in nearly twenty years. I am currently living in Carlsbad. . .*
> *. . .I think of you often, wondering if you are okay. . . what you are doing with yourself. . .*
> *. . .I'd really love to hear from you again. . .to catch up on our lives and to talk about old times. . .*

When Barbara retrieved the letter from her mailbox, she immediately recognized the handwriting scribbled across the envelope. Her heart nearly burst from her chest, yet she remained cautious. It was a week before she gathered the courage to answer Orris.

> *Dear Orris,*
> *I received your letter last week. It was wonderful to hear from you after all these years! How long has it been now? Thirty-five years! Let me see if I can give you an idea of what has been happening in my life. Professionally, I have worked off and on as a dental hygienist. . .*
> *. . .and the year after I graduated from college I married a man I met at Redlands. We have two children. . .after ten years, he asked me for a divorce. . .*

Dear Barbara,
. . .I was married for twenty-three years to a woman I met through a friend at work. We also have two children. . .
. . .Most of the years since I've seen you I worked for a gas turbine manufacturer in San Diego. I am now doing con- sulting work. . .
. . .I'm sorry that things didn't work out for you in your marriage. . .but I'd like to see you again. Would you be inter- ested in meeting for lunch?

Dear Orris,
. . .I have a vivid recollection that may surprise you. The day of my wedding, I drove by your house. When I didn't find you there, I drove over to your father's business. . .I thought you might be working there. . .
. . .I'd love to meet you for lunch. . .

Orris and Barbara met for lunch and the results were fantastic! Old feelings rushed to the surface in their hearts. From then on, each time they met, new revelations about their past misunder- standings came to the light.

"How foolish we were!" Barbara said.

"We were young. . ."

"But if I had only gone to you with what I thought you were saying to me in the letter!"

"I don't even remember the letter you're talking about," Orris added with a chuckle.

"Or, if I had gone to you with what I heard about you!"

"I should have done the same. But we didn't. We weren't very mature, were we? Still, here we are now. . ."

Six months later, on Valentine's Day 1992, Orris presented Barbara with a cuddly white teddy bear.

"Oh, look!" she exclaimed. "It reminds me of all those stuffed animals that used to decorate my bedroom when we were in high school!"

"Did I ever give you any of those?" Orris asked. "I can't seem to recall."

Barbara paused for a moment. "Neither can I! I remember going to the Orange County and Los Angeles County Fairs. . . winning some there. . ."

Orris laughed. "I loved going to those fairs! Hey! Did we ever go together? Do you remember?"

Barbara shook her head. "No. . .I can't remember that, either!"

Orris changed the subject. "Your teddy bear seems to be holding a gift here."

Barbara looked down at the bear in her arms. Between his paws was a red box covered with tiny white hearts. "Oh, how fun!"

"Open the box," Orris urged.

Barbara did. The inside of the box was filled with conversation heart candies.

"Oh, how fun!" Barbara repeated as she reached for one. " 'Oh, boy!' " she read. "This one's for you!"

Orris laughed and Barbara giggled as he reached into the box for another one. " 'My girl,' " he read, then fed it to Barbara with his fingers. "Your turn."

" 'True love.' "

"Mmmm. . .sure is!"

"Oh, Orris, do you remember sharing these in high school?"

"That I remember! Both years, didn't we?"

Barbara nodded. "Both years. Your turn."

" 'Be mine.' "

"Okay!" The couple giggled some more.

Barbara dipped her finger into the box to retrieve another of the sugary sweet candies. Her fingertip brushed against something shiny and hard. "What's this?" she whispered.

Orris didn't have to answer. Barbara knew what it was. The fiery colors of a beautiful engagement ring winked at her from between the pastel colors of the candies.

"Yes! Yes! Yes!" Barbara exclaimed as she threw her arms around the man she had known since fifth grade. . .the man who had walked her home from school. . .the man who had been a part of fond high school memories. . .the man whom she had misunderstood and lost. . .the man who was back in her heart to stay.

July 18, 1992, thirty-six years after their first date, Orris met Barbara at the altar in Eastside Christian Church in Fullerton on the arm of her son, Jim. The wedding party was made up of Barbara's daughters Lynda and Michelle, son-in-law Craig, grandson C. J., Orris's son Mike, who served as best man, both sets of parents, the four sisters of the bride, and high school chums Tom, Charles, Bob, Joan, Louise, Liz, Lynne, and Deanna.

Today the Ansons are committed Christians whose goals are to be continually in the will of God. Together they have led Bible studies, and recently Barbara became a speaker and writer for the Lord.

Each year on Valentine's Day, Orris presents Barbara with a gift of conversation hearts. Though a favorite among children for dropping into Valentine's Day heart-covered sacks, for Orris and Barbara, the candies have never tasted sweeter than they did in 1992.

In the Presence

In the presence of healing,
The pain is not passed on
And at last there is hope
For those who deserved none of the sorrow.
In the presence of healing
There is strange familiarity,
Reconciliation.
At long last, acceptance of old choices;
A wish to call, unannounced, and finally to whisper
To one, to another,
"I was right, after all, to have loved you."

JULIA ARRANTS

The Merchant of Venice

Doug and Lorinda Newton

"I don't know what I'm going to do about Doug," Lorinda Funk complained to an acquaintance. "I'm distressed by the way he keeps following me. He's always sitting near me during church. It's gotten to the point that when I see him entering one side of the sanctuary I go to the other side. In an auditorium that seats over a thousand people, he manages to find me anyway! He's like a puppy going after a treat!"

In September 1989, Lorinda attended Westminster Chapel of Bellevue, Washington, for the first time. She heard about a careers class that was a part of their singles' ministry and decided to check it out. From the moment the twenty-two-year-old brunette was introduced to the class, Doug Newton took notice. For seven months he pursued Lorinda, and for seven months Lorinda avoided him. It finally came down to sharing her concerns with the acquaintance, unaware that the friend would report them to Doug. A few days later, Doug sent a letter to Lorinda, resulting in a phone call from her to him.

"Doug, I really need for you to back off a little," Lorinda said as kindly as she knew how. "I realize you're interested in me. . . I've known it since my first Careers Social. . .but I'm just not ready for a relationship right now."

Six months later Lorinda heard that Doug and his nephew attended a Petra concert. She had been feeling badly for the way she had treated him earlier and felt that he had been good at steering clear of her after the conflict that past spring. Talking to him about Petra, a favorite band of her sister's, was the bridge across the gap.

In early December the Young Messiah tour of 1990 came to Tacoma, about an hour's drive from Bellevue. The Careers class bought a block of tickets and decided to carpool to the concert. Lorinda heard that one of the members, Daryl, was to be one of the drivers and she hoped to get a ride with him. Daryl also happened to be Doug's roommate.

"Daryl, I wanted to see if I could get a ride to Tacoma."

"Sure thing. Another woman from our group is riding with me, too."

Lorinda didn't know it at the time, but that arrangement would place her in the backseat with Doug during the trip and seated next to him at the concert. In spite of the awkwardness, the two enjoyed a pleasant conversation.

On December 17 a snowstorm hit the Seattle area, followed by an Arctic Express freeze. Everything came to a standstill. The Sunday before Christmas, Westminster Chapel canceled its services; the roads were impassable. The leaders of the church created a phone chain to notify members.

As leader of the Careers class, Doug called people in the Careers directory that he knew weren't in the church directory, which included Lorinda. He saved the call to her for last.

The conversation went long. After more than a year of cat and mouse, Doug and Lorinda "hit it off."

"Lorinda," Doug asked, "would you like to attend the New Year's Eve candlelight service with me?"

"Yes, I'd like that."

"How about the Careers party afterward?"

Lorinda laughed lightly. "I'd like that, too."

The courtship of Doug Newton and Lorinda Funk officially began as the New Year rang in.

"Why don't we go down to Oregon and take in some of the Shakespearean plays?" Lorinda suggested to Doug in February 1991.

"I think that sounds like a great idea! But I don't think it would look right for an unmarried couple to go by themselves, so why don't we ask some people in our Careers group to join us?"

Lorinda was thrilled with the idea. "Okay!"

Lorinda and Doug called four of their friends. "If we want to see the plays this summer, we need to go ahead and buy the tickets because they typically sell out." The group purchased tickets for three plays to be performed in August.

"You know, Doug," Lorinda said, "having been an English major in college, I own the complete works of Shakespeare. I think we ought to read the plays before we go to Ashland."

Doug agreed, then purchased copies of the three individual plays that they had tickets for. One of the plays was *The Merchant of Venice*, a play in which the suitors of the heroine Portia, in order to marry her, are forced to select one of the three caskets that her father had prepared. The caskets were gold, silver, and lead. If a man chose the correct casket—the lead one—he won the hand of Portia.

During their courtship, Doug and Lorinda frequently talked about weddings. "Did I ever tell you how I learned about the way my father proposed to my mother?" Lorinda asked.

Doug shook his head, no. "How?"

"In 1985 the furniture store they worked for went out of business. Some of the employees took signs and other store paraphernalia as mementos. My mom wanted the heat vent. When I asked why, she said that my dad had stood over it when he proposed to her."

"So, did she get it?"

"No. The store had been remodeled several times, so it was gone, but that was the first time I ever heard my mother tell that story."

In April Doug made a date with Lorinda for dinner. "I want to take you to Barnaby's."

"The British-style restaurant? We've never been there before. This is a special treat!"

"I hope so. Why don't you wear the floral black jumper you purchased at Nordstrom?"

Lorinda smiled in anticipation. "Okay."

When Doug arrived at Lorinda's, he was handsomely dressed in a dark suit. Lorinda wore the black jumper with a white, short-sleeved blouse. Her hair was held back with a crisp, black hair bow adorned with a large faux pearl encircled in gold on the knot. Doug touched it lightly. "This is how I always found you in the church, you know."

"What do you mean?"

"You always wear big bows in your hair. I'd just look for the bow."

Lorinda rolled her eyes heavenward. Now she knew!

After a deliciously romantic dinner the twenty-nine-year-old bachelor took Lorinda to his home. He led her to the family room where, on the pool table, lay three small boxes: one wrapped in gold paper, one wrapped in silver foil, and one wrapped in aluminum foil (in an effort to represent lead).

Lorinda laughed. She knew that the three boxes represented the caskets in *The Merchant of Venice*. She walked over to the pool table, picked up the "lead" one, and unwrapped it. Inside was a small gold band.

"My grandmother's," Doug said, taking Lorinda by the hand and dragging her over to a heat vent between the family room and kitchen. As he went down on one knee, he asked, "Will you marry me?"

Lorinda was stunned. She had known since February that Doug was the man she'd marry, but she had made a promise to herself as a teenager that she would not accept a marriage proposal until she had dated the man for six months.

"It's only been three and a half months, Doug," Lorinda said quietly. "I have to wait. I told you before about the promise I made to myself. . .I just don't feel ready yet."

Doug stood and nodded. "Then we'll just keep dating. I'll wait for your decision. In the meantime, keep the ring."

Sunday, May 5, Lorinda was to celebrate Mother's Day a week early with her mother. Three weeks had passed since the proposal.

"My mom just got a computer and I thought it'd be cute to get her one of those furry covers for the mouse," Lorinda said to Doug.

"I'll pick you up and take you to Egghead Computer Store. You can get one there."

"Okay. I'll be ready."

Doug picked Lorinda up later that afternoon in his VW Corrado, a sports car designed specifically for the autobahn. As soon as they were comfortably heading down the road, Doug reached for Lorinda's hand as he usually did. He turned his head suddenly as his fingers touched the gold band Lorinda wore on her ring finger.

"You're wearing the ring!" he exclaimed.

Lorinda smiled. As soon as they pulled into the parking lot of Egghead Computer Store, she said, "I've made my decision."

On October 19, 1991, Doug and Lorinda were married at the church where Lorinda had spent her childhood, Newport Covenant Church in Bellevue, Washington.

∞

 $\mathcal{B}$ oth the future bride
and the future groom in Hungary
exchange engagement rings.

∞

Heart's Desire

Harry and Kitty Kunisch

 $\mathcal{D}$ ear Lord, You know my heart," Kitty Donato began a now familiar prayer. "I have chosen wrong before; keep me focused on You. Give me knowledge, wisdom, and discernment when it comes to meeting people, especially men. Yes, Lord, I desire a mate, but I don't want that mate until I am well developed in Your Word. You and I both know that I am so immature (in Your Word) that I wouldn't be ready for a mature Christian man. I don't need to get involved with someone who does not live in You. Only You, Father, know how afraid I am of the opposite sex. Take away my fear when You show me the man You have designed especially for me." Kitty brushed a tear from her cheek, then continued. "Father, the desire of my heart is that he will be a godly man, someone that would study the Bible with me, someone who might possibly want to lead a Bible study with me. Someone deeply involved in the church."

Kitty opened her Bible to Deuteronomy 24:5 and read aloud, " 'If a man has recently married, he must not be sent to war or have any other duty laid on him. For one year he is to be free to stay at home and bring happiness to the wife he has married.' I pray that the man You have in mind for me, Lord, will be a man who has the same desire as that which Your law designed. I also pray, Lord, that this man will feel as I do about possessions: Whatever we own is not ours, but Yours. If someone has a need and we can meet that need, then we gladly give."

Kitty ended her prayer unaware that she had met the man God had designed as her husband. Just a few months previously a friend from church left a message on Kitty's answering machine, in distress. "Kitty you know everyone in church. Do you know Harry Kunisch? My ex and I were friends of his and I've lost contact. Could you get a message to him to call me?"

Who doesn't know Harry Kunisch? Kitty thought as the message continued.

"Would you do something for me, Kitty? Would you try to locate Harry and ask him to call me?"

Kitty followed through on her friend's request. She wasn't sure if Harry would know who she was, but she certainly knew Harry. Harry, a member of the church that Kitty attended, was quite a prayer warrior. Kitty and her granddaughter, Katie, attended services at their multi-service church in Florida twice a week, including Monday evenings when Harry ushered. Whenever Katie, who shied away from everyone, would see Harry, she would run into his arms. This had always amazed Kitty.

A few months passed. Again, Kitty's friend was in trouble, but she was unaware that Kitty knew about her friend's circumstance and that she had been praying. Kitty also knew that the only person she might talk and pray with was Harry.

On Monday evening, due to the seriousness of her friend's circumstance, Kitty desperately searched for Harry. When she found him and told him of the situation, he said, "Let's go to the prayer room and pray together." Together, Kitty and Harry prayed together through the entire church service. When they had finished, Kitty said to Harry, "It's none of my business what happens after this, but my human self needs to know the outcome. Will you follow up with me?"

"I'll be more than happy to," Harry said. His eyes twinkled with a mixture of merriment and compassion.

Harry did follow up and a new friendship began. Shortly afterward, Kitty's mother died. When Kitty returned to Florida after the funeral, she signed up for a class being given at church and was pleasantly surprised to see that Harry was a member of the class as well. Their friendship continued to blossom.

Two months later, in August 1998, Harry asked Kitty to marry him. In his proposal, he said, "I want to take some time off from my duties within the church and I want you to do the same. We should take this time just getting to know one another. I also want you to know how I feel about material wealth. What I have is God's. If God needs something He has loaned to me to be used for someone else, then no questions asked! It's His. Knowing that, Kitty, will you marry me?"

Caught off guard, Kitty's first thought was: *Where is the fear?* Realizing there was none, she answered, "Yes!" Then she grabbed Harry's hand and began to pull him about the rooms of her house. "This is God's house and this is God's stuff! I don't own any of it!"

Two weeks passed before Harry asked, "When?"

"I don't think we should get married without first attending some form of marriage class," Kitty informed him.

The following week, as they opened their church newsletter,

they found an announcement that a marriage class was to begin soon. "Harry, look," Kitty said, pointing to the announcement.

Harry answered with a smile.

"I'll call and sign us up for the class."

"After the class. . .how soon will we be married?"

Kitty, thinking that the class lasted into December, jokingly said, "The first available Saturday after the class ends."

When Kitty called the church to inquire about the availability of the sanctuary, she learned that the Friday after Thanksgiving was open. She and Harry booked the church for that date, then hurriedly began to plan and prepare. Harry said, "You know hundreds of people and I know hundreds of people. I'd hate to have to make a decision of who not to invite." A large wedding was agreed upon.

On Friday, November 27, 1998, escorted behind both of their grandchildren and both of their prayer partners as maid of honor and best man, and on the arms of her pastor and son, Kitty met Harry at the altar. Without fear she pledged her love and life to the man God had designed especially for her, a man who met the desire of her heart.

Place me like a seal over your heart,
   like a seal on your arm;
for love is as strong as death. . . .

SONG OF SOLOMON 8:6 NIV

Do you know you have asked for the costliest thing
Ever made by the Hand above?
A woman's heart, and a woman's life—
And a woman's wonderful love.

LENA LATHROP
from "A Woman's Question"

∞

Family Affair

Frank and Jody Fanizza

Frank Fanizza and Jody Moricca met December 3, 1977, after being introduced to each other by Frank's sister. On January 7, 1978, they were en route to a friend's wedding.

"Did I tell you that I'm getting an apartment with a friend of mine?" Jody asked.

Frank turned his head momentarily, then looked back at the road. "No."

"I'm thirty-one years old, Frank. Living with my sister and brother-in-law has been all well and good, but I think it's time I got out on my own."

Frank shook his head slightly. "I don't think that's such a good idea."

"Why not?" Jody felt a tinge of annoyance.

"Because you will only have to move again soon."

"Move again? Why would I have to move again?"

"You'd have to move when you marry me."

Jody was shocked and didn't fully respond until the next day when Frank and Jody visited with Frank's family. As soon as they walked through the door, she was being hugged and kissed.

"You are exactly what we've been praying for!" they said. "Our prayers have been answered!"

Jody turned to Frank. "You certainly have an odd way of proposing!" she laughed, knowing full well that Frank knew she agreed with his assumption. "Yes, Frank. I will marry you."

Jody and Frank married eight months later on August 12, 1978. They have been growing together in the Lord ever since.

French couples drink the reception toast from
the *coupe de mariage,*
an engraved two-handled cup.

Scorpion Sting

Alex and Dana Chamberlain

Without a scorpion sting, Alex and Dana Chamberlain might never have married. What keeps them happily married, however, is that they share a common goal: to live and work within Christ's will.

Dana Marie Nelson met Alex in June 1980 when she took a summer job at "The Canyon," known to most Americans as the Grand Canyon. Alex had been there for nearly a year as a ministry intern during a year's leave from Princeton Seminary. Although Alex's responsibility was to oversee the summer workers, Dana was assigned to Desert View, thirty minutes from the main village. Therefore, they rarely saw each other. Beyond that, Dana's view of Alex was "nice, but I'm not interested."

By the first week of August, Dana had dated several of the guys in the group and community and was, quite frankly, tired of the whole business. However, she had wanted to dine at one of the area's finest restaurants, El Tovar, which overlooked the canyon. Not wanting to go alone, she asked Alex to be her escort.

"Dutch treat, of course, but we can use my employee discount. And why don't we ask Shirley and Scott. They're good friends, too."

Alex and Dana had a wonderful time! They both flirted outrageously but in jest. After all, they told themselves, this was all in fun. However, the next weekend, as they watched the Pleiades meteor shower together, they realized that something special was happening.

During the next two weeks, Alex made the thirty-minute drive to Dana's post. He brought her bunches of wildflowers, hammed it up when the other workers teased them, and spent hours sharing his thoughts about his life's goals, children, faith, religion, sex, and politics with Dana.

On September 1 Dana and Alex embarked on a farewell hike through the Grand Canyon. The plan was to make a five-day trek, stay with friends and friends of friends in ranger cabins or campgrounds at night, swim in cold pools, and make lifetime memories.

After lunch on the fourth day, Dana lifted her backpack to her leg to hoist it onto her back. "Ahhhhhh!" she screamed, then dropped the pack. Immediately her thigh began to swell around a white puncture mark. Scorpion sting!

Dana hobbled into the ranger hut they were currently using and stretched out on the floor. She held her leg in a viselike grip and moaned. Alex wet bandannas, placed them on Dana's leg, and then hovered anxiously. In spite of herself—and the pain—Dana began to giggle.

"Just my luck!" Alex threw himself into a theatrical pout. "We go on a romantic backpacking trip and you up and die on me!"

"I'm all right!"

"You're delusional!"

"Maybe. But the answer is yes."

Alex paused in his raving. "Uhhhh. . .what was the question?"

Dana struggled to her feet. "I need to soak my leg in the creek to reduce the swelling."

"Come on," Alex said. "Let me help you."

A few minutes later, Dana and Alex sat beside Bright Angel Creek. Dana's leg was submerged in the cold stream and the warm sun shone brightly on their faces. Dana turned to Alex. "Yes."

"Yes?"

"I will marry you. If that's what you've been hinting around."

"Yes?" Alex's smile broke into a grin. Taking Dana's hand in his, he turned to nearby hikers and shouted, "She said yes!"

The first symptom of love in a young man is timidity;
in a girl boldness.

VICTOR HUGO
Les Misérables, 1862

What Treasures Come

Jimmy and Lucy McGuire

Lucy Whitsett picked up the phone in her college dorm room at Mississippi State University and then replaced it on the cradle for the umpteenth time.

"Just call him!" her roommate, Sara, said.

"I can think of dozens of reasons not to," Lucy responded.

"Lucy, the spring ball is fast approaching. You have to invite someone and Jimmy is the boy you want to invite. So, just call him!"

Lucy walked back to the small bed on her side of the room and plopped down on it. "He's one hundred and twenty miles away." Jimmy McGuire was a student at Belhaven College, in Jackson, Mississippi. "He doesn't really have that much going for him. . .he doesn't treat me as if I'm special. . .he's not attentive or particularly well mannered. . .he has no money. . .and. . ."

"And?"

"And he wants to be a preacher!"

Sara sat next to Lucy. "Still, you can't dismiss him from your mind. I think you really like him after all. Why don't you just invite him to the ball?"

Lucy shook her head. "He can't afford to come. It's formal. He doesn't even have a car! How will he get here?"

Sara just smiled as she stood, walked over to the phone, and extended it. "Just call him!"

Within the hour, Lucy had invited him. On the appointed day, Jimmy arrived in his tuxedo and presented Lucy with the prettiest corsage she had ever seen. Multiple miniature red and yellow rosebuds formed a unique and special arrangement, and they matched her gown perfectly.

At the ball, during a break in the dancing, Lucy and Jimmy talked extensively.

"Tell me about what you do to prepare for the ministry," Lucy said.

"I'm the first in my family to even go to college. My parents didn't want me to, so they don't even help. My mother moved and left no forwarding address after I left for school. Just before Thanksgiving break I hitched a ride from Jackson to Atlanta only to discover I'd been locked out. I found a small handwritten note on the door."

"Oh, Jimmy. May I ask what it said?"

"I have moved. I sold everything that was in your room."

"Jimmy, I'm so sorry. That's not a great thing to come home to."

"On a more positive note, Belhaven College gave me voice and work scholarships." He laughed and Lucy noticed that he had a great smile. His eyes sparkled and his grin went from ear to ear. *No wonder he was voted class president,* Lucy thought.

"How did you get here tonight, Jimmy?"

"I hitched."

Lucy looked down at the corsage and lightly touched it with her fingertips. "The roses are beautiful. Thank you again."

Jimmy smiled again. "I made it just for you from roses I picked along a public fence."

It didn't take long before Jimmy's good-natured adaptability to life's circumstances won Lucy's heart. Six months later, standing in Lucy's front yard, Jimmy said, "If our relationship continues to develop as it has thus far, and if you still feel the way you do about me now when you graduate, would you marry me?"

Lucy smiled warmly. "Yes, Jimmy. I'll marry you."

Jimmy didn't have a ring to give to Lucy that day. For the next seven months he saved all he could, even though he was working two jobs and paying for all his own college expenses, to buy an engagement ring. When he had finally saved enough, he purchased the ring which he presented to Lucy one weekend when she visited him at Belhaven. This endeared him to her all the more, but the act that turned the tide in Jimmy's direction over any other young man she dated was a poem he had given to her.

Sometime later, Lucy showed it to her mother.

"Mama, do you know who wrote this? Was it Wordsworth?"

Lucy's mother took the paper the poem was written on and

read it carefully. "I can't say that I know this one. It's so beautiful, though. Let's see if we can't find it in one of our poetry anthologies."

Together they looked, but couldn't find it.

"Jimmy, can I ask where you found the poem you gave to me?" Lucy asked Jimmy the next time she spoke to him.

"I wrote it."

"Oh, Jimmy. . .what precious treasures come in unexpected places."

Yes, they do. . . .

"For Lucy, Peace of Mind"

I sat in silky silence,
my thoughts flew after you
and clutched a fleeting shadow
of things we hope to do;
just me, and just you.

I strained my ears but could not hear
the things my heart found dear. . .
Trust and love, things we share, will
never disappear; no, not from our hearts.

I sat in silky silence,
my thoughts flew after you
And clutched a lasting shadow
of things I knew were true;
for me, and for you.

[Jesus said,] "In my Father's house are many rooms; if it were not so, I would have told you. I am going there to prepare a place for you.

"And if I go and prepare a place for you, I will come back and take you to be with me. . ." JOHN 14:2–3 NIV

- It is believed that the custom of wearing "something blue" began with the ancient Hebrews. In those days the bride wore a "ribband" of blue over her shoulder. This "ribband" represented purity, love, and fidelity.

- In the bride's bouquet, flowers were symbols of virginity, love, joy, beauty, constancy in duty and affection, remembrance, and fertility.

- The Early American bride wore gloves as a sign of modesty and romance.

- Austrian brides are known to wear myrtle in their veils. Myrtle is the flower of life.

- Brides in Belgium embroider their names on a handkerchief, carry it on their wedding day, and frame it as a keepsake.

- A Chinese bride's choice of color for her wedding dress may be red, the color of love and joy.

- In the Czech Republic, brides are still known to carry on the old custom of wearing a wreath of rosemary, a symbol of remembrance.

- German brides save their pennies to buy their wedding shoes.

- Greek brides carry a lump of sugar in their wedding gloves to be certain of a "sweet life."

- Mexican bridal couples are roped with a very large rosary, known as a lasso.

- Brides in Sweden wear three wedding rings, symbolizing engagement, marriage, and motherhood.

PROPOSALS IN ADVENTURE

Darling, my darling, One line in haste to tell you that I love you more today than ever in my life before, that I never see beauty without thinking of you or scent happiness without thinking of you. You have fulfilled all my ambition, realized all my hopes, made all my dreams come true. You have set a crown of roses on my youth and fortified me against the disaster of our days. Your courageous gaiety has inspired me with joy. Your tender faithfulness has been a rock of security and comfort. I have felt for you all kinds of love at once. I have asked much of you and you have never failed me. You have intensified all colours, heightened all beauty, deepened all delight. I love you more than life, my beauty, my wonder.

DUFF COOPER, to the woman he would
one day marry, DIANA (1918)

133

*The bride belongs to the bridegroom. The friend who
attends the bridegroom waits and listens for him, and is full
of joy when he hears the bridegroom's voice. That joy is mine,
and it is now complete.*   JOHN 3:29 NIV

I will always remember the first time he said, "I love you."
It was January 1979. He was chasing me in my mother's
yard. When he caught me, I laughed freely. That's when he
said it. I don't know who was more shocked.

EVA MARIE EVERSON

The Key to His Heart

Rick and Jessie Dalton

Jessie received another e-mail message from her boyfriend,
Rick.

"*I have a secret,*" it read. "*Would you like to know my secret? Do
you have a secret?*"

Jessie all but growled. This had been going on for three days
and she was getting angry. "He has totally lost his mind!" she
said, shaking her head and tossing her thick, blond hair. Then
she grew pensive. "Maybe he's going to break up with me."

She hoped not. In spite of the fact that Rick, who looks amaz-
ingly like Brad Pitt, was far from the romantic sort, he was the
love of her life and it was just a few days before Valentine's Day.

Jessie is a loan processor in the Atlanta, Georgia, area. Her first duty when she arrives at work is to retrieve the customer payments that have been dropped off between closing and opening hours. On February 14, 1996, as she reached down to pick up the night drops that were on the floor, she noticed an envelope with her name on it, in a handwriting that was very familiar to her. As she opened it, a smile broke across her pretty face. It was from Rick.

"Do you have the key to my heart?" the letter read. *"Do you have keys? Where can you get keys? Who has a lot of keys? A locksmith? A policeman? Who?"*

Jessie walked over to her desk, sat down, and read the letter again. She flipped the paper and noticed writing on the back. *"You have until 5:30 this afternoon to find the key."*

Rick is an engineer at Fitel-Lucent Technologies. Jessie knew that he was not available by phone. In fact, she mused, *not* being available by phone was probably part of his plan. He knew that she could not call him and harass him. Jessie, being alone in the office that morning, had only her ingenuity to rely upon.

Jessie grabbed the telephone and dialed the number of a friend. "Do you know anything about this?" she asked.

"No," her friend said, suppressing a giggle. Jessie began to laugh as well.

"This is nuts!"

"He's going to ask you to marry him, Jessie!"

"You've had too much caffeine."

"No! I'll bet he is! He's going to propose to you today; I can just feel it!"

"I don't think so. . ."

"Don't you get it? When he asks you to marry him, and you say yes, that will be the key to his heart!"

"Okay. . .whatever. . .you're no help. I gotta get back to work."

About one o'clock a thought struck Jessie. "The guard at Fitel always has a lot of keys! I'll bet that's it!"

Unfortunately, Jessie was working alone that day and would have to wait until 5:30 (closing time) to leave. Fitel's "guard shack" was a ten minute drive with a total of two four-way stop signs, a red light, and a speed limit of only thirty-five miles per hour. Jessie's emotions were conflicting. "I'm going to kill him when I see him for making me think this hard," she muttered to the steering wheel. Then she giggled. "This is so exciting! And so out of the norm for Rick!"

When she arrived at Fitel, she quickly parked her car and ran to the guard shack where she was met by the guard, a man of about fifty-five.

"Do you have anything for me?" she asked breathlessly.

The guard smiled, retrieved an envelope from a nearby desk, and extended it Jessie. "Don't ask me any questions, 'cause I don't know anything," he told her. "I was just told to give you this envelope."

Jessie pressed her hand to her pounding heart as she returned to her car. She had solved the mystery! When she got in the car and tried to open the envelope, she found that her hands were trembling so that the only unladylike option was to rip it apart. Out fell another key. *Was this the key to his heart?* she wondered.

Peering inside what was left of the envelope, Jessie found another note. It read: *"Okay, so you have gotten this far. I am very proud of you. Now where is the lock for this key? You have twenty minutes to find the lock or it is all over. If you cannot figure it out, you can always go home and think about it. . ."*

Home was twelve very long miles away. Part of the way there, Jessie was forced to put her car on cruise control so that she wouldn't drive any faster than the sixty miles per hour speed limit. The closer she came to her house, the farther away it seemed to be. An eternity later she reached the street where she lived with her daughter, Samantha. As she turned the corner, she screamed out loud, "What in heaven's name is that in my driveway?"

In Jessie's driveway was a ten-foot by four-foot box, wrapped in tin foil and topped with a big red bow. She parked her car and again found herself running toward Rick's shenanigans. Standing in front of the box, she easily spotted two envelopes taped to it. On one was written: *"If you did not find the key, open this one."* On the other was written: *"If you found the key, open this one."*

Jessie grabbed the second envelope and again tore into it. Inside was another key. . .a very small one. She looked at the key, looked at the large box, and looked at the key again. On the front of the box Jessie spotted the tiniest of locks. She slipped the key in and voila! The lock released and a door came open. Jessie took a step, peeked in, and saw nothing.

"What?" she said aloud, to no one. "Two people could fit in this thing and there's nothing in there!" Jessie took another step and glanced up. There it was. . .way up high. . .stuck to the top of the ten-foot box. . .a small bag with hearts and ribbons all over it.

Jessie, who is by no means short, was forced to jump. . .jump . . .jump up and rip it down! When she opened the bag, she found a little box. With shaking hands, and a not-so-steady heart, she pulled back the top and blinked hard. A beautiful diamond ring winked back.

Suddenly Rick was behind her. "Well, you gonna marry me or what?"

On May 4, 1996, with their children Samantha Powell, Kellyn, Seth, and Jacob Dalton attending them, Rick Dalton and Jessica Powell became Mr. and Mrs. Rick Dalton.

I love you,
Not only for what you are
But for what I am
When I am with you.

True Love

I love you,
Not only for what
You have made of yourself
But for what
You are making of me.

I love you,
For the part of me
That you bring out;
I love you,
For putting your hand
Into my heaped-up heart
And passing over
All the foolish, weak things
That you can't help
Dimly seeing there,
And for drawing out
Into the light
All the beautiful belongings
That no one else had looked
Quite far enough to find.

I love you because you
Are helping me to make
Of the lumber of my life
Not a tavern
But a temple;
Out of works
Of my every day
Not a reproach
But a song.

ROY CROFT

Couples in Bermuda plant a small tree in their lawn, where it grows tall and strong, a symbol of the growth of their marriage. In Switzerland the same tradition is celebrated. A pine tree is planted, a symbol of fertility.

My Girl

Vic and Kelly King

October 28, 1987

For some reason I keep thinking about marriage and just what God wants in a marriage. I'm not even dating anyone, but yet it seems I've become obsessed with thoughts about it. I don't know whether God is preparing me for something or if this is something I'm just going through. I'm really confused!

I keep thinking about Vic King—a guy from P.C. West who went on our singles' hayride last week. I'd really like to go out with him, but I doubt he'll give me the time of day. All I know is that he has a lot of the qualities I look for in a guy. If anything, it reassures me that there are guys like Vic who are still single and have a heart for the Lord.

I do feel like I'm ready to meet that special someone. I just need to be patient on the Lord and let Him control the timing. First of all I need to give it to Him and strive to be the godly woman God wants me to be! Praise God for answered prayers and I claim the victory in this area of my life!

Kelly Kennedy had known Vic King for years. They had grown up just miles from each other in Oklahoma City, and both

True Love

attended Putnam City West High School (though they graduated three years apart). Vic had been a very popular student. He played football, was vice president of his senior class, and had a reputation for being one of the nicest guys in school. Kelly was a shy teenager and had only known Vic from "afar." In fact, she knew his younger brother Gary better.

After high school, Vic graduated from the University of Oklahoma, then moved to a small Oklahoma town where he worked as a youth minister. Kelly graduated from Oklahoma Baptist University, then returned to Oklahoma City and a job as a marketing director for a financial institution. A few years passed when Vic, who loved youth ministry but was not keen on small-town life, moved back to OKC and began working for the Hertz Corporation. It was during this time, at a friend's wedding, that Vic King and Kelly Kennedy were reintroduced. A few months later, after her church's singles' group hayride, Kelly scribbled in her personal journal about seeing Vic again.

> . . .*Not that I have any thoughts about getting married. . .*
> *or even dating at this time. I am just placing my life in Your*
> *most capable hands. You can work out the rest.*

God must have rubbed His mighty palms together and said, "Okay, then! Let's see what we can do here! Both Vic and Kelly are excellent skiers. I think I'll plan a ski trip. . ."

Kelly smiled when she saw that Vic's name was on the list of singles slated to go on the upcoming singles' group annual ski trip. Kelly had almost not gone—she was very busy at work—but at the last minute decided to attend.

The group went to several ski resorts in Colorado. On their first day out, Kelly asked Vic, "Can I ski with you?"

"You can if you can keep up," Vic replied casually.

Skiing with Vic was fun, and a couple of days later Kelly told the girls in her cabin, "I know that Vic is the man I'll marry."

140

"How can you know that?" they asked.

"I don't know. . .don't ask me why. . .I just feel like he's an answer to prayer."

During that week, Vic began to show an interest in Kelly. Romance had begun to blossom in the cold, crisp Colorado air.

Valentine's Day arrived, offering Vic a fine opportunity to show Kelly his adventurous nature. Vic secretly drove to Kelly's home, killing his headlights before the house came into view. He rolled to a stop in front of her home, quietly slipped out of his car, ran up to the front door where he hid a gift for her, then ran back to his car. Moments later he was pulled over by the police for driving suspiciously in the neighborhood without his headlights on. It took some fast talking and a call to Kelly to get him out of trouble.

In March 1988 Vic and Kelly went to Angel Fire, New Mexico, with Kelly's mother and father for a long weekend of snow skiing. The group was disappointed at the conditions—or lack thereof—so early one morning, Kelly, her father, and Vic traveled an hour and a half to Taos in hopes of finding better slopes.

While Mr. Kennedy and Vic sat in the front seat, Kelly sat alone in the back. (Mrs. Kennedy stayed behind at their condo in Angel Fire.) As the car swerved up and along the winding mountainside road, Kelly noticed that Vic had some sort of string hanging out the front of his parka, but a tinge of carsickness kept her from asking about it.

As soon as the threesome arrived in Taos and parked the car, Kelly jumped out and took a deep breath. "Ah! Smell the air! Gorgeous day! Gorgeous place!" Taos had long been a favorite place of Kelly and her father. For the rest of the morning Kelly, Vic, and Mr. Kennedy enjoyed skiing together, especially relishing the area around Kachina Bowl on the back side of the mountain.

"I'm taking a black slope," Vic suddenly called out, indicating the most difficult slope.

"Dad and I will stay on the blue," Kelly returned.

Vic nodded and left father and daughter to ski the easier of the slopes. Later, when they reached the chairlift, Kelly remarked to her father that Vic had not arrived. "Looks like we've been separated. Oh, well. We'll meet up later."

Unbeknownst to Kelly, Vic had taken a wrong turn. This left him somewhat panic-stricken because today was the day he intended to propose, and his well thought-out scheme—to tie signs up on the chairlift so that Kelly would see his proposal as they rode it together—was falling apart.

An hour later, Vic found Kelly and her father at the base of the mountain, ready to ride the lift again.

"What's wrong?" Kelly asked. "You seem a little flustered."

"Nothing. . .nothing. . .just relieved to find you. That's all."

"Okay. No big deal. I knew all along we'd meet up at the end of the day."

"Yeah. . .ready to go back up?"

Kelly nodded. Her father had already begun his ascent.

As they rode the lift back to the top of the slope, Vic began the most pathetic attempt at singing "My Girl" that Kelly had ever heard. It was off key but full of gusto so that everyone could hear. When they reached the top of the lift and jumped from their seats, Vic pulled Kelly aside, then pulled a folded sheet of vinyl from his pocket.

"What is this?"

"Open it. . ."

As Kelly unfolded the sheet, bright green words began to appear.

KELLY, WILL YOU MARRY ME?

Vic took off his skis and knelt down before Kelly, whose attention was diverted by a small crowd that had gathered farther up the mountain. In the center stood Kelly's father, with his camera, recording the moment. Kelly began laughing, fought to gain composure, and then answered the age-old question.

"Yes!" she exclaimed. The crowd above clapped and cheered.

But they did not see Vic give Kelly a ring. True to his creative and romantic nature, after they returned to Oklahoma City, Vic designed a scavenger hunt for Kelly. The mad search led Kelly to Vic's house where her ring was hidden in a pack of gum that had been buried in the front flower bed.

The happy skiers married July 16, 1988, in Oklahoma City, Oklahoma.

"Will You Love Me When I'm Old?"

I would ask of you, my darling,
A question soft and low
That gives me many a heartache
As the moments come and go.
Your love I know is truthful
But the truest love grows cold.
It is this that I would ask you,
Will you love me when I'm old?

Life's morn will soon be waning
And its evening bells be tolled,
But my heart shall know no sadness
If you'll love me when I'm old.

When my hair shall shade the snowdrift
And mine eyes shall dimmer grow

True Love

I would lean upon some loved one
Through the valley as I go.

I would claim of you a promise
Worth to me a world of gold.
It is only this, my darling,
That you'll love me when I'm old.

AUTHOR UNKNOWN

On a whim we drove to a deserted beach in Galveston, Texas. We parked his truck, got out, and walked along the moonlit beach. Our hands were clasped. . .we were walking. . .not talking. . .enjoying the company of each other. As the weather turned chilly (it was January), we went to a park bench to snuggle and get warm. We began talking about our past lives, our future, and our dreams, plans, and expectations. As our conversation came to an end, he quietly asked, "Will you marry me?" I accepted his proposal: to live a life filled with love, dedicated to each other, our future children, and his son by a previous marriage. That was nearly twenty years ago. The beach, though changed, is still our favorite place to go in January, when the weather is cold and the surf is up and there's no one there but us. A trip taken on a whim ended in a marriage bond of strength, perseverance, change, growth, discovery, friendship, and—most of all—love.

CAMILLE HORTON

High Above the World

Dennis and Christy Peters

Christy Peters is a wisp of a young woman; there couldn't be more than ninety-five pounds to her and most of that is eyes. Her thick, medium-brown hair shines and bounces near her shoulders as she talks about the second love of her life, her husband, Dennis. One is with Christy for only a short time before one knows that her first love is God.

When Christy speaks of the magical, adventurous day that Dennis proposed, she does so in animated vivaciousness. It's a story too good to keep to herself, with a testimony that will forever remain a blessing to all those who hear it.

Christy had known Dennis for a long time. They were in the same college ministry at Northland, A Church Distributed, in Orlando, Florida, where Christy is the child-care coordinator for the church and Dennis plays acoustic and electric guitar for the worship team.

One afternoon Christy was praying. . .talking to the Lord about her future husband. "You pick my husband," she told Him. "I want a godly man for my children, someone who will raise them in You, should something happen to me, someone who will raise them in Your Word and Your truth."

Unexpectedly, God laid Dennis on her heart. "But, Lord," she immediately responded, "I'm not attracted to Dennis. It's not that Dennis is not a nice guy, or that he's not good-looking. He's wonderful, but he's not what I imagine when I daydream about my Prince Charming!" Christy took a deep breath and exhaled slowly. "But I know," she continued, "that if he is the right man for me, You can change that."

Oddly enough, a week later Dennis and Christy had their first date, and yes! she was attracted to him! Not being one to beat around the bush, she boldly told him during their first date that she had prayed about her future husband and that the Lord had told her that Dennis would be him. To Christy's shock, he didn't head for the nearest exit. Instead, he said, "Well, He hasn't said anything to me about that yet."

"I know the Lord has to confirm it in your life, also."

Dennis and Christy dated for eleven months, and in that time Dennis introduced Christy to opera. She loved it and often thought—though she never said anything to Dennis—it would be fun to go to the Metropolitan Opera House in New York City. In fact, the two places that she always wanted to visit were New York City and Europe.

Unbeknownst to Christy, Dennis had the idea of surprising her with a trip to New York City to visit the opera. He discussed it with a woman where he worked—someone who was familiar with the city—and with Kathy Wallace, the church administrator for Northland, A Church Distributed.

In spite of careful planning, though, Dennis wasn't able to get the tickets. He decided to drop the whole idea, but Kathy talked him into taking Christy anyway.

"There's other things to do, Dennis!" Kathy exclaimed. "There's more to New York City than just opera!"

And so, Dennis planned this most wonderful day.

"I've got a surprise for you," Dennis told Christy. "I want you to be ready to go somewhere with me on Saturday."

"Where?" she asked excitedly.

"I'm not telling you. Just be ready by six o'clock in the morning. I'll pick you up then. And dress nice, but comfortably. We'll be outside a lot."

We're going to Disney World again, Christy thought. *The last time he had a "surprise" for me, that's where he took me.* So for her special day, Christy dressed in a casual, simple, long denim dress (Dennis's favorite), suitable for warm weather and comfortable for walking on the hot asphalt streets at Disney.

True to his word, Dennis rapped on Christy's bedroom window at six o'clock Saturday morning. They got in his car and as he drove he encouraged her to tell him a story. . .not that either of them now recalls what it was about. In her usual manner, Christy became so involved in what she was saying that she didn't notice any of the signs for Orlando International Airport. It wasn't until they parked in the parking garage that she shouted, "We're at the airport!"

Dennis grinned.

"Dennis, it's too expensive to eat and shop here."

"We're not here to eat and shop."

Hand in hand, Dennis and Christy walked into the airport and right up to the ticket counter. Dennis suppressed a smile as Christy's mouth fell open. Dennis had purchased tickets! Though he tried to keep her from seeing where they were going, Christy caught a glimpse of their destination printed on the ticket. Newark, New Jersey, it read.

"What in the world are we going to do in Newark?" Christy asked.

Dennis remained silent.

As they stepped into the terminal in Newark, a driver holding a sign with Dennis's name printed on it met them near the gate. *I can't believe what is happening to me!* Christy thought. As they were escorted to a shiny beige Lincoln Town Car, her heart pounded with excitement. *This is the day! He's going to ask me to be his wife today!*

Newark is just a stone's throw from downtown Manhattan, and though the happy couple didn't get to hear the opera, they did see the Opera House. Their driver took them on a tour of Manhattan: South Street Sea Port, Rockefeller Center, St. Patrick's Cathedral, the Metropolitan Museum of Art, Macy's, and Saks Fifth Avenue! Everywhere they went, the driver waited patiently. Between sites, he told them about his recent heartache; he and his longtime girlfriend had broken up, and he was very sad.

"I know this is a difficult time," Christy told him. "But I also know that God has someone very special for you." And then Dennis and Christy shared with him how they met and that God was the center of their relationship.

They ate lunch in Central Park's Tavern On The Green.

"It is so beautiful here!" Christy exclaimed as they later walked around the park. Their driver took them to other places of interest until it was time for dinner.

The previous excitement Christy had experienced paled in comparison to her discovery that they were dining on top of the World Trade Center at Windows On The World restaurant, a restaurant with an outside wall of windows that overlook the city. From where they sat, the two young lovers could see the skyline as it lit up. They looked down and gazed across New York Harbor to see the Statue of Liberty.

"This is incredible!" Christy said. She was so happy. . .so enthralled with the moment. . .that she didn't care that she was still in her walking-around clothes. To this day, she can't even remember what they ate!

After dinner, before dessert, Christy excused herself to go to the ladies' room. While she was gone from the table, she thought about how all that day, while Dennis and she were touring the city, he had held her left ring finger gently between the fingers of his right hand.

When Christy returned to the table, Dennis stood up, then came to her side of the table. He held her chair as she sat down, but instead of returning to his chair, he got down on one knee, took her left hand in his, slipped the ring he had been carrying around with him all day on her finger, and said, "Christy, will you marry me?"

Dennis had asked their waiter to take a photo of them with the camera they had brought to capture their special day. He wasn't too thrilled about doing it, until Dennis got down on one knee and he realized what was happening. Then his face broke into a huge smile! Everyone at the tables around them watched and smiled as Christy exclaimed, "Yes!"

After dinner, when Dennis and Christy went back downstairs to their waiting driver, she bounced up and down as she showed him her ring. "I just love you!" he said happily. "Let me show you more of the city!"

"We have a time limit," Dennis explained to him. "We have to get back to the airport in time for our flight."

"You aren't spending the night?" he asked, surprised.

"No," they told him. "That would be against what Jesus taught us."

The driver was truly shocked at their testimony for the Lord and their feelings about the sanctity of marriage!

The magical day in New York City did come to an end, but their flight home was equally romantic. The plane was fairly empty; there were possibly only five others on the plane. "This is like having a private jet," Christy whispered in the silence.

"There's a final surprise waiting for you," Dennis whispered back.

"What?"

"You'll see."

When Dennis and Christy returned to Orlando and got in the car, Dennis put a personally made CD in the CD player. It was filled with their favorite songs and songs that had a message about their lives together. Between each song, Dennis had recorded himself quoting Scriptures that reflected what was in his heart.

The last song was Out of the Grey's "Dreaming of April," a song that was played in April 1998 when Dennis and Christy became Mr. and Mrs. Dennis Peters.

Finnish brides wear crowns of gold. After the wedding, the bride is blindfolded and unmarried female guests dance around the bride. Whoever receives the crown is believed to be the next in line for matrimony.

⚭

I Remember You

Eddie and Karen Johnson

Karen Berry wasn't looking for romance when she signed up for a two-week free membership on Matchmaker.com (the Christian Connection) web site. The native of Kokomo, Indiana, who lived and worked in Nashville was more accurately seeking Christian men and women of faith with whom she could communicate. She had truly been blessed thus far. She had taken a trip to Atlanta to formally meet a couple of women she had been writing, and had become friends with several women in (ironically) Nashville that she met through the site. But she wasn't looking for romance. . .

Then came January 15, 1999, and an e-mail from a cute little blond-headed guy named Eddie Johnson.

"I read that you are from Kokomo," he wrote. "Although I'm living in Dallas now, I am from Kokomo, too! My parents still live there."

Karen wrote back: "My parents still live there, too. Where do your parents live?"

Eddie's return e-mail indicated that their parents lived only ten minutes from each other. "Which high school did you attend?" he asked in a subsequent e-mail.

Karen's answer revealed that she had attended Northwestern High School and that, being older than he, she would have graduated six years before Eddie.

"I graduated from Kokomo Christian," Eddie responded. "But my sister dated a wrestler from your school who graduated the same year as you. I used to attend the matches with my sister."

Karen responded: "I have to imagine that our paths crossed at some time then! I was a cheerleader for the wrestling team so I'm sure you saw me jumping around. . .chanting, 'Wrestle, wrestle, wrestle! Twist 'em like a pretzel!' Did I tell you that when I was a senior I worked as a waitress at Pizza Hut?"

"No kidding!" Eddie wrote back. "My friends and I used to frequent the joint! You probably waited on us more than once, I imagine! This is a little off the wall, but, growing up, who was your doctor? Mine was Dr. Fretz. He actually brought me into the world at St. Joseph's Hospital."

"What a small world!" Karen wrote back. "Dr. Fretz delivered me, too, in the very same hospital!"

After a season of trading e-mails back and forth, Eddie and Karen decided to talk by phone. A fun and exciting three weeks went by before they took the next step. "I'm flying to Nashville," Eddie told Karen. "I think it's time we really meet each other."

With one step from the plane, Eddie won Karen's heart; he was carrying a single red rose. Over the weekend the two hometown natives became "reacquainted." Shortly thereafter, Karen flew to Dallas. "Isn't it funny? We grew up in the same hometown but didn't truly get to know one another until we were miles and miles apart."

Eddie laughed. "At one time we could have driven to each other's homes in minutes. Now we have to take a plane."

It was merely three months later that Eddie made a life-changing decision. "I'm moving to Nashville," he told Karen.

"You're kidding! Really?"

"No, I'm not kidding. I think it's time I courted you properly."

For a woman who wasn't looking for romance, romance was what Karen got. A little over seven months later, with many conversations about marriage behind them, and at a singles' party (with several friends present), Eddie Johnson turned to Karen Berry at the stroke of midnight, January 1, 2000. "Karen, I want to spend the rest of my life with you." He got down on one knee, took her left hand in his, slipped the diamond ring that her father had proposed to her mother with on her finger, and said, "Karen, will you marry me?"

Karen felt her eyes misting over as she pulled Eddie up and kissed him several times. "I would love to be your wife!"

"Hey, everyone!" Eddie exclaimed moments later. "I just asked Karen to marry me and she said 'yes!' Kind of ironic seeing as I just accepted the job of Director of Singles and Small Groups for the church!"

Everyone laughed and congratulated Karen and Eddie. "Wouldn't it have been funny," Eddie said later, "if we had known back in Pizza Hut what we know now? You would have come up to my table and said, 'May I take your order?' and I would have said, 'Yeah, I'm only thirteen, but in about twenty years, will you marry me?'"

"I'll give you one better," Karen replied. "You and I started our lives in the same hospital. One day, many years from now, we'll end it together."

Eddie nodded. "That we will," he agreed. "That we will."

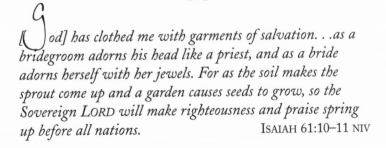

[God] has clothed me with garments of salvation. . .as a bridegroom adorns his head like a priest, and as a bride adorns herself with her jewels. For as the soil makes the sprout come up and a garden causes seeds to grow, so the Sovereign Lord will make righteousness and praise spring up before all nations. ISAIAH 61:10–11 NIV

True Love

I give you my hand!
I give you my love, more precious than money,
I give you myself before preaching or law;
Will you give me yourself? Will you come travel with me?
Shall we stick by each other as long as we live?

WALT WHITMAN

∞

Nothing Wasted

Dave and Jane Aldrich

Jane, are you free this weekend?" Jane's sister, Blanche, asked.
Jane shifted the telephone to her other ear. "What do have
in mind?"

"I need a fourth person for a game of Crazy Eights after dinner. One of the soldiers from Ft. Benjamin Harrison is coming
over after church for dinner and a game of cards. If you're free,
I'd like for you to join us."

"Sounds good. Which soldier is it this time?" Blanche and
her husband lived across the street from the fort, so having the
soldiers over after church for dinner and a game of cards was a
common practice.

"Dave Aldrich. He's very shy, but my dinners snag him every
time!" Blanche laughed.

On a cold February afternoon in 1967, Dave Aldrich and Jane
Edwards sat at Jane's sister's dining room table with Blanche and
her husband, Don, playing a game of Crazy Eights.

"Dave, what do you do for the army?" Jane asked.

"I'm taking advanced training."

"Really? In what?"

"I'm in Special Forces, trained in communications."

"That sounds interesting," Jane said with a smile, noting just how quiet the young soldier was.

In spite of Dave's shy character, he managed to ask Jane out for a date. Over the next few weeks they went out about six times before Dave was shipped out to Okinawa, Japan, where he served as the Communications Specialist for the Voice of United Nations.

"Write me?" Dave asked.

"Absolutely."

"I'm going to be gone a long time, most likely over a year."

"I'll write."

Dave was right. He was in Japan for a year and a half before he returned to the States and was stationed at Ft. Bragg, North Carolina.

"It's a long way from Indianapolis," Dave commented.

"Yeah, but I'm from Tennessee, so this is good training for you!" Jane joked. "You need a little southern culture!"

"We'll see each other when we can, okay? It may be only once every three or four months, though."

"We'll call them marathon dates," Jane concluded.

The marathon dates were just that. At the beginning of the weekend, Dave and a buddy would go to a car lot to "try out" a car for the weekend, then head north to Indianapolis. It was on one of those weekends that Dave asked, "Will you marry me and go to Africa?"

Jane was stunned. She had been hoping for the proposal, but the part about Africa was never included in her daydreams. "What? Why Africa?"

"Ever since I was sixteen years old I have felt called by God to become a missionary. After my stint in the army, I'm going to apply to ELWA."

"ELWA? What's that?"

"ELWA is a mission stationed in Monrovia, Liberia."

"South Africa?"

"Yes. I want to work with their radio stations to get the gospel out into the bush."

"That's commendable, Dave, but I'm going to have to pray about this. I come from a big southern family, you know. We're kinda funny about hearth and home."

"I understand completely. I don't want you to do anything you feel you cannot do. But I know this is the direction that God is calling me to, and I feel that He put you in my life to be my wife. At the same time, I know that it's your decision."

Three months passed. Every day Jane prayed. "Lord, You know that I love Dave. But do I love him enough to go to the ends of the earth with him? Because that's exactly what he's asking me to do, You know! Can I leave everything that is near and dear to my heart to go clear around the globe? And, if we do go, Lord, what do You have in store for us? I appreciate the fact that Dave wants to serve You, but why can't we serve You here, in the United States?"

Eventually Jane's prayer became more simple. "God, just give me peace in my heart. If Dave is the man You have for me, then I leave the rest of our future in Your capable hands."

God did just that. On June 11, 1970, Dave and Jane joined hands, hearts, and their futures and became one in the eyes of God and man. They moved to Oregon, where Dave enrolled at Multnomah School of the Bible so that he could obtain the Bible credits necessary for ELWA's mission program.

In the spring of 1972, Jane shared special news with Dave.

"I'm pregnant," she said. After the initial excitement, Jane whispered what had been on her heart. "How will this affect things? What about our plans to go to Africa?"

"We'll just pray about it," Dave answered. And they did.

It was but a few months later that President Tubman, president of Monrovia, Liberia, died. Politics in South Africa changed drastically. The country no longer allowed missionaries to enter and asked those who were already there to leave.

Dave and Jane, two willing vessels, never made it to Africa. However, over the past thirty years they have served God in many ways. For several years Dave worked as a television producer for *The Gary Randall Program,* a Christian talk show that aired five days a week. For the past ten years he has been the general manager of Event Rental. Jane worked as an office manager for a consulting engineering firm. Together they sang in various choirs (Dave served as a choir director for a little church in Gresham, Oregon), taught Sunday school, were leaders in the Christian Ambassadors, and organized youth events.

In the stillness of a cool, Oregon evening, Jane whispered to Dave, "God certainly has blessed us. I don't feel that anything was wasted. We have two wonderful children and have lived to enjoy our two grandchildren. It's Psalm 128, all rolled up into our lives. God is faithful."

Blessed are all who fear the LORD,
who walk in his ways.
You will eat the fruit of your labor;
blessings and prosperity will be yours.
Your wife will be like a fruitful vine within your house;
your sons will be like olive shoots around your table.
Thus is the man blessed who fears the LORD.

May the LORD bless you from Zion
all the days of your life;
may you see the prosperity of Jerusalem,
and may you live to see your children's children.
Peace be upon Israel.

PSALM 128 NIV

True Love

The Little Brown Church

Tim and Mindy Wall

Friday, December 19, 1991, was Tim Wall's twenty-seventh birthday. His girlfriend, Mindy, had an intimate dinner for two planned and was anxiously looking forward to it. Those plans were thwarted when Tim announced, "For my birthday I'm taking you up to John and Becky's house."

"What!" Mindy exclaimed. "Tim! I've got a nice dinner planned for you. In fact, I've planned the whole evening. Dinner for two, a walk down Christmas Tree Lane in downtown Fresno."

Tim appeared to be understanding but wasn't budging in his plans. "I've already told them we are coming."

"I've only met these people once before and you want us to spend your birthday with them?"

"It is my birthday. . ." Tim trailed off.

Mindy was stumped for a comeback. "Well, okay. If that's what you want."

Mindy had met Tim when she began attending a new church in Fresno, California, in September 1990. One evening after services she asked the pastor, Jim Akin, about joining the choir.

Jim craned his neck and looked around. "Tim!" he called out, upon seeing Tim Wall. "Come here for a minute, please."

Tim walked over. "Tim, you're in the choir and Mindy is interested in joining. Mindy, why don't you have Tim take you over and show you around?"

"I'd be happy to." Joining the choir turned out to be a very good thing; Tim and Mindy had their first date at the choir's Christmas party shortly thereafter.

Nearly a year later, on December 19, 1991, Tim and Mindy were on their way to Hume Lake Christian Camp, about an hour and a half from Fresno, where John and Becky Moore lived. "We're not going hiking, are we?" Mindy had asked a few days before, knowing how Tim loved hiking at Hume Lake.

"No, no. Just dinner with John and Becky."

"Because I'm planning on wearing dress shoes, but if we're going hiking. . ."

"Just dinner."

"I know how much you like to go to the Little Brown Church."

The Little Brown Church was just that: a dollhouse—one foot by two feet by three feet—just big enough for a Bible and a notepad. The Little Brown Church was a lovely spot for spending time alone with God and was a favorite place of Tim's.

Tim and Mindy had no sooner arrived at John and Becky's than Tim said to John, "I have the prescription that you wanted me to pick up."

"Great!" John replied. "Let's go ahead and go to the pharmacy."

Mindy was somewhat frustrated. She didn't know Becky Moore well enough to carry on any type of lengthy conversation with her, and she wondered how they would spend the time while Tim and John were gone.

"So, how was the drive up?" Becky asked.

"Good."

"I hope you like Mexican food."

"I love Mexican food."

"How old is Tim today?"

"Twenty-seven. Do you like living up here?"

"Oh, yeah. It's nice and quiet. . ."

The small talk continued until Tim and John returned.

After dinner Tim said to Mindy, "Let's go look at the Little Brown Church."

"What? Tim, are you trying to kill me? You told me we weren't hiking and I wore heels. I'll break my neck."

Tim wrapped his arms around Mindy and nuzzled her neck.

"Ah, come on. It's not so far. We drove really close. Please?"

Mindy laughed lightly. "You are trying to kill me, but I love you, so okay. Let's go."

The snow and ice made the steep slopes up to the Little Brown Church more hazardous. Using a flashlight to guide them, Tim pulled Mindy along; all the while she was thinking, *He is trying to kill me.*

Once they arrived, Tim said, "Let's see if the Bible is still in there." He reached in and pulled out a white rose. "Look! Someone left a rose in here. Oh! It has your name on it!" Tim handed the rose to Mindy.

"Let me see! Tim, hold the flashlight still." Mindy and Tim were both laughing. When he brought the flashlight's beam to rest on the card, Mindy read: "Mindy will you. . ."

Mindy swung around. Tim was before her, kneeling in the snow. She burst into tears, then wrapped her arms around him and kissed him. "Yes. Yes." Tim pulled Mindy away from him, then slipped a ring on her finger.

"Let's go back and tell John and Becky," Mindy suggested.

"No need," Tim said. "They were in on it all along."

The tradition of carrying the bride
over the threshold began in ancient Rome.
A stumble at that moment
was considered unlucky.

For two days I have been asking myself every moment if such happiness is not a dream. It seems to me that what I feel is not of earth. I cannot yet comprehend this cloudless heaven.
                                                    VICTOR HUGO,
                                          just after his engagement to
                                  ADELE FOUCHER had been announced

She is coming, my own, my sweet;
were it ever so airy to tread,
my heart would hear her and beat,
were it earth in an earthy bed;
my dust would hear her and beat,
had I lain for a century dead,
would I start and tremble under her feet,
and blossom in purple and red.

ALFRED, LORD TENNYSON

One Eye on the Girl
Dr. Luis and Pat Palau

On an evening in the fall of 1960, on the campus of Multnomah Biblical Seminary in Portland, Oregon, Luis Palau walked toward the home of a friend where a class party was to be held. The twenty-six-year-old exchange student from Argentina noticed a group of fellow classmates, namely females, walking on the other side of the street. "Are you going to the party?" he called over.

"We sure are!" they returned.

Luis sprinted over to them and, without reason, looked specifically at Pat Scofield and said, "Can I walk with you?"

"Sure."

Luis had noticed Pat before but hadn't felt anything special toward her. She dressed well—stylishly—but other than that. . .

"So you're from Argentina?" Pat asked, more as a statement than a question.

"Yes. I've been here for about six months."

"Does your family still live there?"

"My mother and my five sisters. My father died when I was ten years old."

"I'm so sorry," Pat responded kindly.

"What about you? Do you have brothers and sisters?"

Their conversation continued as Luis and Pat arrived at the party with their classmates. They weren't "together" at the party, but a chord of interest had been struck within Luis. He saw Pat as being fun and talkative, mature and stylish. He was impressed with her spiritual sensitivity most of all.

Soon, Luis began to look for Pat on campus. When he learned that she studied in the school's library, he quickly made the location his place of study, too! While there, however, he had one eye on the book and one eye on the girl. "I don't know what's come over me," Luis confided to a friend. "I only know that I think about Pat a lot. But I also know that I have big plans and that I have to take care of my mother back in Argentina. I want to preach the gospel around the world!"

"And where does Pat fit in to all this?"

"That's just it. I don't know! And I don't think she even knows how I feel about her."

Finally Pat did catch on and they began to see each other.

Nothing serious had developed, but Luis was smitten. Just before Christmas break Luis told Pat how he felt. "I want you to know, Pat, that you are special to me, that I care about you a great deal, and I hope we can spend more time together after the holidays."

"I'd like that, Luis. I really would."

Luis's second semester was exciting for him, something that Pat could take credit for. They spent as much time together as possible. Pat could take credit for something else as well. "My grades are slipping," he teased her. "I have a C in my Romans class."

"What's that going to do to your grade point average?"

"Bring it down a tenth of a point, I'm afraid."

Just before the Valentine's Day banquet, Luis and Pat walked together in the cold Portland rain, sharing an umbrella and conversation.

"My family has endured great poverty for several years in Argentina. I want to make certain that they are taken care of."

Pat nodded but remained silent.

"Pat, will you return to South America with me?"

Pat stopped walking and turned to Luis. It wasn't "the" question, but she knew what he meant. "Yes, I'll return to South America with you."

Luis placed his arm around her shoulder and began to walk again. He knew what her "yes" meant, as well.

Multnomah Bible College had a policy that kept Luis and Pat's engagement unofficial since first-year students were not allowed to become engaged.

However, a ministry opportunity with OC International came up at the end of the summer of 1961. Luis and Pat would need to speed up their wedding plans so that they could move to Detroit in order to make the seven-month training for it.

"I need to talk with you about Pat Scofield and me," Luis told the school's president. "We were planning to become officially engaged, but we want to attend training for this ministry opportunity."

"You know the school's policy," the president said. "But I will take it into consideration."

Eventually, the school permitted Luis and Pat to move forward with their plans. In the eyes of the school, they were still unofficially engaged, but they were allowed to make plans and send invitations for an August 5 wedding.

On August 5, 1961, Luis and Pat married at Cedar Mill Bible Church in Portland, Oregon. During more than thirty years of mass evangelism, evangelist Luis Palau has spoken to hundreds of millions of people in 104 nations through radio and television broadcasts, and face-to-face to thirteen million people in sixty nations. He and Pat have four grown sons and live in Portland, Oregon.

After nearly forty years of marriage, he still keeps one eye on the book and one eye on the girl!

*F*ar too often, our lives become overburdened with trivialities, myriad small projects, which at the time seem so terribly important. Soon, these chores become more important than the truly important things in life—family, faith, lending a helping hand to those who are less fortunate. It takes a great deal of effort to keep from being consumed with the daily comings and going, but it's a goal which we all should strive toward. We should take the time to hold hands, to say a kind word now and then, to be polite and giving and sharing. More important, we should take the time to get back to the basics of life—love.

BIRCH BAYH

I'm Going to Disney World!

Patrick and Carissa Dunn

September 30, 1999, Carissa Connelly and her boyfriend, Patrick Dunn, returned to her apartment after a trip to the laundromat.

"Well, just another Tuesday evening spent in the laundromat," moaned Carissa, the personal assistant to Marita Littauer, president of CLASServices, Inc., and also an inside sales representative at Hosanna, Faith Comes By Hearing.

Patrick moved toward the stereo in search of a CD to play. "At least our clothes are clean," he teased.

Carissa walked into her kitchen and began to rummage through the pantry in search of something to eat. "Patrick, I need a change of scenery!"

The words were familiar to Patrick; Carissa repeated them often. He smiled as he moved to stand in front of her, gathered her hands in his, and said, "Honey, are you willing to take a big risk and trust me?"

Carissa's surprised eyes responded to her usually conservative boyfriend. "Risk? What do you mean? I've been dating you for a year and a half, and you've never said anything remotely close to this. . ."

"Are you willing to really, really trust me?" Patrick responded to Carissa's question with a question. "I promise that it's nothing bad."

"Okay. . .yes. . ."

"Okay, then. I need you to trust me and follow some instructions. Honey, let's pack your bags because we're flying somewhere tomorrow!"

"But I have to go to work—"

"I've already gotten permission from your boss."

Carissa let that piece of information sink in before she asked, "What do I need to pack?"

"I'll tell you exactly!"

The next day Patrick and Carissa flew from Albuquerque to Orlando where a luxurious transport bus took them straight to the Polynesian Resort at Disney World. Waterfalls and lush gardens greeted the pair as they departed at the deluxe resort where Patrick had reserved two rooms.

"I've dreamed of going to Disney World all my life!" Carissa exclaimed.

Patrick smiled. "I know."

"How are we able to do all this?"

"For me, it's business." Patrick, the host and co-producer of a Christian music video program, 24Seven Videos, answered truthfully. "To be honest with you, honey, you and I are attending a VIP-only media event for Disney's Millennium Celebration. Only a few thousand people have been invited."

During their stay, Patrick and Carissa were pampered beyond belief! "I can't get over how well we're being treated!" Carissa remarked. For three days Patrick and Carissa combed Disney World and took on the attitude of children. They played in the theme parks as if they didn't have a single care.

"Is this heaven?" Carissa asked.

"No!" Patrick joked. "It's Disney World."

On their last morning, Patrick and Carissa walked out onto the end of a pier overlooking a beautiful lake surrounded by a white sand beach. The view was nearly breathtaking. Carissa leaned into Patrick and nudged with her elbow. "Hey, Snail. Wouldn't this be the perfect place to ask me?" She gently nudged again, then looked up into his blue eyes and smiled. Patrick had consistently said that theirs would be a three-year courtship.

Patrick turned to Carissa and returned the smile, then got down on one knee. As if by the magic of Disney, a ring box suddenly appeared.

"Carissa Noel Connelly, will you marry me?" He opened the box and the warm Florida sun caught the prism of a solitaire diamond, sending a rainbow of love to Carissa's heart.

"Are you serious, honey? Really?" Carissa bit her lip to keep from exploding.

"Yes."

Carissa took a deep breath. "Yes!"

Patrick stood and the two embraced. Against a backdrop of fairy tales, all disbelief left Carissa and was replaced by the beautiful reality.

*This is what the L*ORD *says. . .there will be heard once more the sounds of joy and gladness, the voices of bride and bride-groom, and the voices of those who bring thank offerings to the house of the L*ORD, *saying, 'Give thanks to the L*ORD *Almighty, for the L*ORD *is good; his love endures forever. . . .' "*
JEREMIAH 33:10–11 NIV

Love makes up for the lack of long memories
by a sort of magic.
All other affections need a past;
love creates a past which envelops us as if by enchantment.

BENJAMIN CONSTANT DE REBECQUE

Fringe Benefits

Bruce and Carol Williamson

Before Bruce Williamson and Carol Dunn ever had their first date, they established "type of date guidelines." An "A" date meant coat and tie, a "B" date was business/casual, and a "C" date was an invitation to wear jeans or shorts, casual shirts, and sneakers. Their first date was a "B" date: dinner at a restaurant called Hamilton's.

As soon as they were seated and the water glasses placed before them, Bruce, an airline pilot, presented a card and rose to Carol.

"What's this? What does the rose mean?" Carol asked.

"On each date I will add a rose until you have a dozen."

Carol smiled warmly. "What happens once I have the dozen?"

"I'll ask you to marry me," Bruce teased.

After seven dates (and roses), the pressure began to build. "I am thinking we should bring the roses-thing to a halt," Carol suggested.

"I feel the same way," Bruce agreed.

A few dates later, however, Bruce began to hear the anticipation of a proposal in Carol's voice. He wanted to surprise her, so he invited her out on a "B" date. Surely, he reasoned, she would expect a proposal only during an "A" date.

Secret reservations were again made for Hamilton's. Bruce arrived at Carol's home at seven o'clock. Once they were in Bruce's truck and headed down the road, Carol turned to ask, "Where are we going?"

"It's a surprise. I'm going to play a cassette tape I made for you. Don't say anything. Just listen."

Bruce had carefully timed ten songs so that as they drove into the parking lot of the restaurant, "Can You Feel the Love Tonight?" was playing.

As soon as they were seated, the manager of the restaurant presented Carol with a dozen roses. Five minutes later, the manager returned to the table with a wrapped package.

"Open it," Bruce said quietly.

Carol complied. Inside the box was a card on which Bruce had written: "When I said I loved you, I meant forever." Under the card was folded tissue paper. When Carol carefully separated it, she saw a t-shirt. Printed on the front was "Marry me and Fly Free!"

Carol looked up. "Do you know what this says to me?"

"Yes. I'm asking you to marry me."

Bruce opened the ring box he had kept hidden and extended it to Carol.

Brief moments passed. Finally she said, "Yes," then reached over and gave Bruce a hug and kiss. Patrons of the restaurant clapped in happy ovation.

"So I was wondering," Bruce said with a grin, "what you're doing January 15, 2000."

Carol giggled. "Marrying you."

The tradition of the honeymoon began in ancient Norway. Unlike the vacations we have today, a Norwegian's honeymoon was a matter of life and death. Indeed the happy couple hid away for a few days, but the groom was actually hiding from the bride's father! In those days the custom was for the groom to "steal" the bride by capture. After about a month, when things had quieted down, the couple returned to the village to begin their lives together. The word "honeymoon" comes from the Norse *hjunottsmanathr*.

*Jacob was in love with Rachel and said [to her father],
"I'll work for you seven years in return for
your younger daughter Rachel [as my wife]."*

GENESIS 29:18 NIV

• Dearly beloved, we are gathered together here in the sight of God, and in the face of this company, to join together this man and this woman in holy Matrimony; which is an honourable estate, instituted of God, signifying unto us the mystical union that is betwixt Christ and his Church: which holy estate Christ adorned and beautified with his presence and first miracle that he wrought in Cana of Galilee, and is commended of Saint Paul to be honourable among all men: and therefore is not by any to be entered into unadvisedly or lightly; but reverently, discreetly, advisedly, soberly, and in the fear of God.

from the *Book of Common Prayer*

- We are here to celebrate and share in the glorious act that God is about to perform—the act by which He converts their love for one another into the holy and sacred estate of marriage. This relationship is an honorable and sacred one, established by our Creator for the welfare and happiness of mankind, and approved by the Apostle Paul as honorable among all men. It is designed to unite two sympathies and hopes into one; and it rests upon the mutual confidence and devotion of husband and wife. May it be in extreme thoughtfulness and reverence, and in dependence upon divine guidance, that you enter now into this holy relationship.

  from the *Zion Wedding Ceremony*

- In the name of God, I. . .take you. . .to have and to hold from this day forward, for better or worse, for richer or poorer, in sickness and in health, to love and to cherish, until we are parted by death. This is my solemn vow.

  from *Episcopal Church Exchange of Vows*

- Christ calls you into union with Him and with one another. I ask you now in the presence of God and this congregation to declare your intent. Will you have this man to be your husband, to live together in a holy marriage? Will you love him, comfort him, honor and keep him in sickness and in health, and forsaking all others, be faithful to him as long as you both shall live?

  from the *United Methodist Church Declaration of Consent*

- I will be faithful to you and honest with you; I will respect, trust, help, and care for you; I will share my life with you; I will forgive you as we have been forgiven; and I will try with you better to understand ourselves, the world, and God; through the best and the worst of what is to come as long as we live.

  from the *Lutheran Marriage Vow*

- Entreat me not to leave you, or to return from following after you, for where you go I will go, and where you stay I will stay. Your people will be my people, and your God will be my God. And where you die, I will die and there I will be buried. May the Lord do with me and more if anything but death parts you from me.

  from the *Traditional Exchange of Vows*

- You now have what remains the most honorable title which may exist between a man and a woman—the title of "husband" and "wife." For your first gift as husband and wife, that gift will be a single rose. In the past, the rose was considered a symbol of love and a single rose always meant only one thing—it meant the words "I love you." So it is appropriate that for your first gift—as husband and wife—that gift would be a single rose.

  from the *Rose Ceremony*

ROMANTIC PROPOSALS

How do I love thee? Let me count the ways.
I love thee to the depth and breadth and height
My soul can reach, when feeling out of sight
For the ends of Being and ideal Grace.
I love thee to the level of every day's
Most quiet need, by sun and candlelight.
I love thee freely, as men strive for Right;
I love thee purely, as they turn from Praise.
I love thee with the passion put to use
In my old griefs, and with my childhood's faith.
I love thee with a love I seemed to lose
With my lost saints,—I love thee with the breath,
Smiles, tears, of all my life!—and, if God choose,
I shall but love thee better after death.

ELIZABETH BARRETT BROWNING
Sonnet XLIII: "How Do I Love Thee?"

All glorious is the princess within [her chamber];
her gown is interwoven with gold.
In embroidered garments she is led to the king;
her virgin companions follow her and are brought to you.

PSALM 45:13–14 NIV

From "I love you" to the proposal was a month. From the proposal to the wedding was six days. From the wedding to eternity is bliss. EVA MARIE EVERSON

Flower petals have been a part of the wedding ceremony for many years. England's time-honored tradition is the procession to the church, led by a small girl throwing petals for the bride to walk upon. In India, at the completion of the ceremony, the brother of the groom sprinkles flower petals on the bride and groom.

Dedicate yourself to the call of your heart
and see where it leads you.

UNKNOWN

True Love

Valley Wide

Doug and Gail Jenner

In 1969 Gail Fiorini was a sophomore at California State University in Chico, California. Chico, the second oldest campus in the California State University school system, has sprawling grounds where Romanesque architecture mingles with modern buildings, and Big Chico River snakes through the green grasses and under canopies of trees. Gail's freshman year had been spent in one of the student dorms located on the rambling campus. During the year she made arrangements for her sophomore year to move into an apartment with another student.

That plan fell through.

"I need a place to live," Gail told the sister of an old boyfriend. "The girl I was supposed to live with moved away and didn't come back."

"I need an extra roommate!" Carol informed her. "I'm living with three other girls on the first floor of an old, two-story house and we have room for one more!"

Gail soon moved in with Carol, Susan Jenner, Arleen Hayden, and Bonnie Hayden. Though Gail had known Carol previously, as time went on she formed a closer relationship with Susan, Arleen, and Bonnie, cousins from Scott Valley, California.

By anyone's definition, Scott Valley is a small, remote mountain valley town nestled near the Oregon border, surrounded by wilderness. For Gail, "back home" was the city in southern California where a young man named Michael waited for her return.

"Michael and I have an agreement. While I'm away, we're going to date others. But naturally it will just be casual dating," Gail told her roommates.

"Do you think you'll marry Michael?" Arleen asked.

175

"Oh, absolutely! But right now I'm young and carefree and we've both agreed to date other people."

"But do the guys you date here know about Michael?"

"I preface *all* my dates with 'I have a boyfriend and have no intention of getting serious about anyone else.' " Gail shrugged. "It's an arrangement that can work."

Susan smiled. "My brother Doug is dropping by in a little while. Gail, he says he met you at a big barbecue last year."

Gail shook her head. "I don't remember him."

"You wouldn't. He's too shy to come right out and talk to you. He's a senior this year. . .lives about two miles from here in an apartment."

It was a few weeks into the term when Susan asked Gail if she would be interested in going out with her brother Doug.

"He has curly hair and talks funny!" Gail exclaimed, thinking to herself: *And he's all country while I am from the city.*

But when Doug came by the house, he and Gail talked, shaking Gail's aversion to dating the young cowboy.

"Doug still wants to date you," Susan teased several weeks later.

Gail smiled. "Okay. . .okay! But be sure to tell him that I have a boyfriend back home!"

To be safe, Gail repeated the worn line to Doug on their first date.

"Okay," he replied shyly. "That's fine."

Doug introduced Gail to things she had never experienced before—the rodeo, hiking in the woods, fishing at the river—things she found herself enjoying more and more. They only occasionally went out to dinner or to a movie. As time marched on, Gail visited Susan and Doug's family at their ranch in Scott Valley where Doug chauffeured Gail around in fine style: on the back of a tractor or in an old pickup truck. Chores became dates. The unlikely couple moved irrigation lines from field to field, plowed, fed the cows and pigs, or picked apples for cider.

The following summer, Susan invited Gail to join her family on a five-day mountain pack trip.

"I dunno, Susan. I've only been on a horse a few times. . ."

"You can do it!"

"But this is a *real* pack trip. . .high into the Marble Mountains. . .hours on a horse!" Deep down, however, Gail was so excited she could hardly contain herself.

Gail rode at the back of the line of horses, which gave her ample opportunity to watch Doug. *He's so quiet,* she thought, *so rugged. . .so very, very handsome!* Gail was falling in love, but she wasn't about to admit it to anyone. . .not just yet.

One afternoon during the pack trip, Gail and Doug sat on a large boulder and fished in a crystal clear creek. The water played a gentle symphony, the birds sang a sweet song, yet everything else was quiet.

"What's it like to live your whole life in one place?" Gail asked.

"I'm fourth generation on the ranch. It's hard, ya know. A lot of sacrifices."

"For instance?"

"There's a lack of freedom. Not a lot of time for play."

Gail nodded in understanding. "It's different in the city."

"That it is. A rancher's work is never really done." He paused, then added, "But it's a good life."

"But it would be hard. . .to move. . .you know, from the city to the country."

Doug's eyes met hers. He didn't respond. He didn't have to. But Gail's mind was racing. *He's so different from anyone I've ever met before! He's serious, but he knows so much about animals. . .and life. . .and he doesn't try to impress anybody. . .*

The next fall Gail was faced with a difficult situation. She and Susan continued to share housing (although they had two new

roommates) and Chico had a new student: Michael, Gail's
boyfriend from the city.

"To be close to you," he informed her.

The dilemma grew complicated: Gail was so torn she would
literally leave a date with Michael and then go out with Doug.

"What are you doing?" Susan exclaimed in a warning voice.
"Don't you think you ought to choose?"

"I know that I should, but I can't! Michael's come all this
way to be with me. . .I've been dating him for *four years!*"

Even Doug's roommates got involved. "He's in love with
you, Gail. Every time you two go out, he ends up in the bathroom throwing up," they told her.

Truth be told, Michael or not, Gail could not get Doug out
of her head. . .or her heart.

One evening, after taking Gail out to dinner, he added
another factor.

"I'm in love with you, Gail. Remember the night I saw you
at the barbecue?"

Gail's food was stuck in her throat and her heart hammered
in her ears. "Not really, actually. . ."

"I went home that night and told the guys in my apartment
that you were 'the one.' I knew it then, Gail, and I'll be honest
with you. I can't stand sharing you anymore. I thought I could
do it, but I can't. When I get home from our dates I'm as sick
as a dog, my nerves are so shot."

"I just can't decide, Doug! I care about you both! Really, I do!"

Doug stood from his seat and tossed his napkin on the table.
"Then this is it. I'm not going on like this. You stay with
Michael. But don't think I'm going to call. I'm not. I've got to
get over this and just go on."

Gail was stunned, but she managed to convince herself that
everything would be all right. "Oh, he'll call," she told herself.

But he didn't. . .and he never did. Should they run into each other, Doug was kind but quiet. Gail was devastated. Soon she concocted reasons to "stumble" into him or to "run over to Doug's apartment."

Michael was becoming suspicious. He knew that Gail had been dating Doug and that she liked him as a person, but he had no idea what Gail was truly going through.

Several weeks went by. One afternoon Gail said to Susan, "I don't know what to do!"

A pleading-for-help phone call home resulted in her mother advising, "Honey, still waters run deep. This guy knows what he wants. He's not a boy. He's a man. He knows what he can handle and he's not going to be played with. He's serious."

Gail nodded in agreement, then took the step she needed to take. She called Michael. "I need time, Michael."

"How long do you need?"

"I don't know yet. . ."

During winter break, Susan invited Gail to join her and her family for New Year's Eve. Gail accepted the invitation and went up to the valley where a large group joined together to celebrate the coming new year. It was pitifully obvious that Doug was "sick" over his and Gail's parting. Friends and family shared their concern. But hope for Doug was just hours away.

"I've asked Michael for time," Gail told him when they were alone.

"Really?"

"Mmmhmmm."

Doug shifted slightly. "How do you feel about me, Gail? Are you serious about me?"

Gail paused, but only for a moment. "Yes," she whispered. "But I'm scared silly. I don't know what the future holds. I've built my whole life around the idea of marrying Michael. . ."

When the night was over, she and Doug were officially "exclusive." Gail was finally able to admit to herself that she was in love.

"I can't stand not being with Doug," she told Susan. "I feel safe, contented, loved, and adored."

A weekend in February at the ranch sealed their fate.

Doug had to work on the ranch a good deal of that weekend. One afternoon Gail donned jeans, a sweatshirt, hat, gloves, and boots and took a walk in the glistening snow. She stopped by the shop where Doug was working alone, their first time alone all weekend.

"Cold out," Gail remarked.

"Yep." Doug, covered in grease, smiled at her. "But I'm glad you came to see me." He resumed his work on a farm tractor.

Gail stood close enough to watch Doug work without being in his way. "What are you doing there?"

"Repairing this tractor."

"What's wrong with it?" Gail crossed her arms and peered around Doug as he continued his work.

"It's almost spring. Time to start farming soon so I got to get the equipment ready."

"You smell like oil," Gail said with a smile.

Doug again stopped long enough to return it, then turned back to his work. "Let me explain what I'm doing. See, first ya gotta. . ."

Gail could see his mouth moving, but couldn't hear the words. Her thoughts were too loud. *He's so rugged. . .so handsome. And so very humble and kind. I don't think he truly realizes how creative and intelligent he is.* Gail glanced around the shop. *What would it be like if I married Doug? If I saw him in this environment every single day for the rest of our lives together? Life would be so different. But in a good way. Challenging. . .interesting. . .*

Suddenly Doug dropped his tools and turned to look at Gail. In an instant locked between seconds and eons, their eyes met. He took the necessary steps to reach her, wrapped his arms around her, and gave her a passionate kiss. "Marry me," he whispered when they broke for air.

Gail laughed and cried at the same time. "Yes!"

"What?"

"Yes! But don't tell anyone yet! I have to talk to Michael."

"Okay, then." Doug nodded, then kissed her again.

"I feel like I've come home," Gail whispered as Doug bent to kiss her again. "I'm where I belong."

Talking to Michael was the most difficult thing Gail ever had to do. The months had left everyone a little scarred; both Michael and Gail cried.

"I care more about you than I do about trying to hang on to something that isn't going to work," Michael said through his tears. "You've got to do what you've got to do."

That was 1971. Doug and Gail Jenner continue to live in Scott Valley where their children are the fifth generation born on their cattle ranch. Their home is the original homestead, circa 1860s. Scott Valley is only thirty-five miles long and six miles wide.

But it's big enough for Gail.

The Passionate Shepherd to His Love

Come live with me and be my love,
And we will all the pleasures prove
That valleys, groves, hills, and fields,
Woods or steepy mountain yields.
And we will sit upon the rocks,
Seeing the shepherds feed their flocks,
By shallow rivers to whose falls
Melodious birds sing madrigals.

And I will make thee beds of roses
And a thousand fragrant posies,
A cap of flowers, and a kirtle
Embroidered all with leaves of myrtle;

A gown made of the finest wool
Which from our pretty lambs we pull;
Fair lined slippers for the cold,
With buckles of the purest gold;

A belt of straw and ivy buds,
With coral clasps and amber studs:
And if these pleasures may thee move,
Come live with me and be my love.

The shepherds' swains shall dance and sing
For thy delight each May morning:
If these delights thy mind may move,
Then live with me and be my love.

CHRISTOPHER MARLOWE
(1564–1593)

[My boyfriend's] family and I attended a Bill Gothard Christian family seminar where we were taught that a man should never approach a woman to discuss engagement without the father's permission. This is also an old Italian tradition, and we are all Italian. On my twenty-sixth birthday I went to my parents' house for dinner and was surprised when I found Jim already there. I did not suspect anything until I entered the kitchen. There I found my mother humming and almost giggling. In the living room, Jim and Dad were sitting there. . .looking strange. Finally Jim asked me into the summer patio. His exact words escape me. . .I was in shock. . . . My father was proud that Jim had shown the respect to ask him first for my hand in marriage before he asked me. It was the right thing to do and very romantic, too! We married Thanksgiving weekend, 1981.

FRANCINE FAZIO

Enjoy life with your wife, whom you love,
all the days of this meaningless
life that God has given you under the sun—
all your meaningless days.
For this is your lot in life and in your
toilsome labor under the sun.

ECCLESIASTES 9:9 NIV

True Love

Request Line

Rob and Joy Elder

"Where is she?!" the keyboard player for the six-time Dove recipient Steve Green mouthed to Dr. Rob Elder in the middle of a concert in St. Louis, Missouri.

Rob was in a panic. His girlfriend, Joy Hoedel, had left her front row seat to go get some popcorn. But Rob had expected her back before now. Now he threw his hands up, shrugged his shoulders, and then bolted down the aisle to the concession stand where he found his girlfriend calmly waiting in line.

"Get back to the concert!" he insisted as he pulled her away from the line.

"What? What's going on?"

"Just get back to the concert!"

Joy, the marketing director for radio station KSIV in St. Louis, had long been a fan of Steve Green. Because Rob had never listened to his music, she had been thrilled when he told her that he would attend the promotional concert Joy was required to work. She had been even more pleased when he volunteered to help Steve's crew with the setup. Unbeknownst to Joy, Rob did more than set up the equipment; he set up a romantic evening as well.

Moments after the two returned to their seats, Steve spoke to the audience. "This is the part of the show where I ask for requests. Is there anyone who has a favorite song they'd like to hear this evening?"

Rob raised his hand. Joy nudged him. "You don't know any of his songs," she whispered as the cameras swung to focus on their front row seats and their images appeared on the screens over the stage.

184

" 'Household of Faith,' " Rob called out.

Joy was visibly relieved. *Great choice,* she thought.

"Are you married?" Steve asked as he stepped off the stage and then walked to the front row.

Joy smiled. "We're planning to be someday."

At that moment, in front of a concert hall full of people and with all the cameras on him, Rob stood, dropped to one knee, and said, "I love you and I'd like you to be my wife. Will you marry me?"

Joy sat speechless! She opened her mouth, but nothing came out.

"Well?" Steve interrupted. "What are you going to say?"

"Uh. . .uh. . .sure!"

Rob presented Joy with a beautiful pear-shaped diamond ring, but when he tried to put it on her hand, it wouldn't fit. Steve took it from Rob's hand, held it up to the camera, and chuckled. "Maybe this ring will fit someone else!"

The crowd "ooh'd" and "aah'd" as the diamond flashed across the two screens.

"You're putting it on the wrong hand, Rob," Steve continued jovially. "Try the left hand this time." An embarrassed Rob quickly slipped the ring onto Joy's left ring finger. It fit perfectly!

"Congratulations," Steve said, then began to sing his well-known Christ-centered song on marriage, "Household of Faith"!

Joy linked her arm through Rob's, listening in awe, right up to the last note. She looked down at her beautiful new ring, then to her awesome husband-to-be.

Who needs popcorn?

Household of faith

We'll build a household of faith
that together we can make.
And when the strong winds blow;
it won't fall down.
As one in Him we'll grow
the whole world will know
that we are a household of faith.

BRENT LAMB AND JOHN ROSASCO

∞

The Kidnapping

Rob and Heather Avery-Clyde

"She's different," Rob Clyde expressed dramatically to his mother. "Mom, Heather's the kind of girl you'll want me to marry. . .and she's gorgeous, too!"

In the fall of 1989, Rob Clyde was a freshman at George Mason University in Fairfax, Virginia. A few years earlier he had met Heather Avery at Domino's in Sterling, Virginia, where they were both employees. But their friendship had only been casual. The closest they had ever been was in Rob's junior and senior years at Park View High School when he and Heather sat next to each other in Spanish 1 and Spanish 2. His "name" was Julio and her "name" was Elena.

The summer of 1992 would change their casual relationship into something special. Though she was dating someone she knew from Virginia Tech (a college from which she would later graduate with a degree in theater arts), Heather spent the summer "hanging out" with Rob. At summer's end, it was time for Heather to return to school.

"I'll drive you back," Rob volunteered. "I can drive you and your stuff back and help you move into your dorm."

"Sure. Okay. That'd be nice." Heather wasn't thinking that her college boyfriend, Nic, might literally be waiting for her, but he was. As soon as Rob and Heather walked into her dorm room they came face-to-face with Nic.

"Welcome to the O K Corral," Heather muttered under her breath as the theme song from *The Good, the Bad, and the Ugly* played in her head.

The two young men continued to do battle with their unblinking eyes until Nic took a step toward the opened door.

"I'll talk to you later," he told Heather. She knew she would soon have to make a decision.

The six-foot, one-inch Rob turned to the petite woman standing next to him. "So that's Nic?" he asked.

Heather smiled sheepishly.

Heather sat in the middle of her dorm bed with her palms up in front of her. "On the one hand," she began, pretending to weigh the imaginary scales, "we have Rob. On the other, we have Nic. Rob. Nic. Rob, who spent the entire summer with me, expressing a valiant interest in getting to know me, fully aware that Nic existed. Nic, whom I didn't see all summer. Rob, whom I did fun things with. . .like climbing the tree in front of the Washington Monument on our second date. . .Rob, who comes from a great home and has a great family and Nic, who has a somewhat checkered past. Rob, whom I would most likely be happy with on a long-term basis, or Nic, whose past life foretells future problems." Heather threw her hands up. More than all that, Rob's relationship with Jesus was impressive, even though Heather was not yet a Christian. Rob's heart belonged to Jesus, and Heather's now belonged to Rob.

"My sorority is having a Christmas party," Heather told Rob. It was three years later, the last week of November. "I'll be going with a friend of mine from school."

"Okay," Rob replied casually. His mind was racing, however. The party was the perfect opportunity for a well-thought-out plan. As soon as he could, he called his brother Benji and his friend, Kim Poncin. "Here's the scoop. . .," Rob began, ". . .and if everything goes well, the night of the Christmas party is the night she agrees to marry me."

"And if not?" Kim asked with a smile.

"It could turn out messy!"

The day of the party arrived. Rob worked his air shift at WTCN, a small AM radio station where Rob wore several hats, quickly drove home, grabbed the pear-shaped diamond ring he had purchased a month earlier, then drove to a nearby florist where he purchased a dozen red roses. By five P.M. he met Kim and Benji, who were clad in jeans and denim shirts and holding Lone Ranger masks and Dick Tracy derby hats, at Kim's apartment. Rob gave the long white box of roses to his two co-conspirators, then gave them the thumbs-up as they climbed into Benji's car and began a four-hour drive to Blacksburg, Virginia, where Heather prepared for a party, unaware of what the night would hold for her. Rob returned to Kim's apartment to "wait."

Three hours later Kim and Benji arrived at the Roanoke Airport where they got in a white stretch limousine that Rob had ordered. They were chauffeured to The Hokie Grill in downtown Blacksburg, Virginia, where the Christmas party was well underway. As they slipped out of the limo, they put the masks and hats on, grabbed the roses, and walked inside.

"Halloween's over, guys!" they heard the gawking patrons of The Hokie Grill call out. Without responding, they continued onward until they spotted Heather, who was beautifully dressed in a short-sleeved, box neck cocktail dress. Without saying a word, they handed her the roses and a card that read: *Your presence is requested by R.C.*

The willing kidnap victim followed the two masked marauders out of the restaurant to the waiting limousine without realizing that she was leaving her coat, purse, and date at the party! Once they were in the car and the driver pulled away from the restaurant, Rob's helpers began to play the first of four tapes that Rob had previously recorded for Heather. On these tapes, Rob reminisced about the past three years of their relationship, recorded music that was important to the two of them, and tried his hand at subliminal persuasion.

When the threesome arrived back at the airport, they left the limo and returned to Benji's car. Within minutes they were heading up Route 81 to Sterling, Rob's tapes continuing to entertain and persuade. Upon their arrival Heather was blindfolded so that she could not see the final destination in Rob's plan. By four o'clock Friday morning, everyone, Kim, Benji, Heather, Rob, and Benji's brother Dan (who had been entertaining Rob) had arrived in Washington, D.C.

Dan helped the blindfolded Heather from the car, then led her down a small hill and through the dirt and rocks that surrounded the Washington Monument.

"Sit, Heather," Dan said quietly, then gently pushed her toward a cold cement bench. "Don't take off the blindfold."

As he walked away, he heard Heather yell, "Don't leave me!"

Within seconds Rob was there in front of her. Tenderly he removed the blindfold. Without saying a word, he handed her the jewelry box he had been hiding for a very long month. Heather took it. . .opened it slowly. . .and found it to be. . .empty!

With the Washington Monument behind him, and underneath a tree that they had climbed on their second date almost three years earlier, Rob immediately dropped to one knee and extended the pinkie of his right hand, displaying the sparkling diamond ring. His voice quivered as he said the simplest, most difficult words of his life. "Heather, will you marry me?"

Nine months later, September 16, 1995, Heather Avery became Mrs. Rob Clyde in an afternoon ceremony at Floris United Methodist Church in Herndon, Virginia.

That I may come near to her, draw me nearer to Thee than to her; that I may know her, make me to know Thee more than her; that I may love her with the perfect love of a perfectly whole heart, cause me to love Thee more than her and most of all. Amen. Amen. That nothing may be between me and her, be Thou between us, every moment. That we may be constantly together, draw us into separate loneliness with Thyself. And when we meet breast to breast, my God, let it be on thine own. Amen. Amen.

TEMPLE GAIRDNER,
prayer before his marriage

Precious Moments

Jose and Lorimar Ayala

For Jose Ayala, it's a matter of dates, and he remembers them all well. On August 10, 1996, mutual friends introduced him to Lorimar Vazquez. Jose was employed at Baker's, a shoe store in the Altamonte Mall in Altamonte Springs, Florida. Lorimar was employed by Twisted Silver, a jewelry store in the same mall.

Even though they were young—both juniors in high

school—they knew almost instantly that there was something special between the two of them. Jose, however, was a shy young man who was unsure of the manners of dating.

Each evening, after work, Jose walked Lorimar to her car in the employee parking lot where they would talk for a while before saying good-bye. On September 17, 1996, as Jose and Lorimar talked by her car, she reached over and kissed Jose. It was their first kiss.

The next day, September 18, Jose purchased a Precious Moments figurine for Lorimar: a little boy, down on his knee, extending a flower to a little girl standing before him. After work, when he saw Lorimar, he gave her the gift, then asked her out for their official first date.

By December 1997, Jose knew that Lorimar would be the only woman for him. In his heart, he saw her as his future wife and the mother of his children. Best of all, she was a godly woman, pure and chaste.

May 31, 1998, just before he and Lorimar graduated from high school, they were honored at their church (along with the other high school graduates) in a special ceremony. When the ceremony was over, Peter Vivaldi, pastor of Centro de la Familia Cristiana (Center of the Christian Family), said, "Jose needs to say some words."

Jose discreetly pulled the ring that he had been hiding out of his sock. Lorimar was, thankfully, oblivious to his action. He cleared his throat and began to speak what his heart had been singing for nearly six months. "I want to thank my family and friends and especially God for this moment. I want to ask, with the permission of Lorimar's parents. . .," Jose turned to the beautiful woman who stood to his right. She was sobbing, almost uncontrollably, as Jose got down on one knee. The pastor's wife came to Lorimar, wrapped her in her arms, and helped to hold her up. Jose continued. "Will you marry me?"

The congregation of nearly a thousand people applauded as Lorimar answered, "Yes." Grown men cried.

It was July 3, 1999, a hot, humid Florida afternoon, when Jose heard the most precious words of his life. On that date, with those words, his precious lady became his much-adored wife.

$\mathcal{S}$panish brides receive thirteen coins from their grooms. This symbolizes his ability to support her. The coins are to be carried by a young girl during the ceremony.

The Lost Boy and Tinkerbell

Randy and Linda Jones

Randy featured his proposal in *The Glennville Sentinel*, Glennville, Georgia, on July 29, 1999:

$\mathcal{D}$earest Linda,
Remember when we were shopping together and I said, "Linda, I love you very much, and would you mind if I told the world?" And you said, "No, I would love it!"

When we first met in Savannah at that little shop, Creations of the Heart, I realized that you were someone special. I have learned, since then, that your strength of character, your intelligence, and beauty are blended within a personality that is a testament to the attention God gives to His daughters. I believe angels have brought us together.

I LOVE YOU!

True Love

Your most endearing quality is your playfulness. You are like Tinkerbell to me, the Lost Boy. You have brought joy to every facet of my life. You are magical!

With you, will be my every moment.
Toward you, will be my every movement.
You will be to me,
My Sweet Gravity,
My future, my past, my present
Manifest Destiny.

How will I love thee?
With all my heart and soul and mind and more—
with all my time!
With words of Webster and the world and with imagined rhyme!
For peace, contentment, harmony, as one, like Two Bells—
a Perfect Chime.

I promise to be a faithful servant to our God.
I promise to be with you. I'll try never to be more than an
    arm's length
    Away and to answer your needs at the speed of thought.
I promise to give you my time, to join our families into one
    new family,
    To love yours as I love mine.

Bees gather pollen and so do butterflies.
Both according to the will of God.
It is my suggestion that we follow the butterflies.

Dearest Linda,
Before God and Glennville,

WILL YOU MARRY ME?

Linda's reply was also featured in *The Glennville Sentinal,* Glennville, Georgia, August 19, 1999.

Darling Randy,

Together every moment—
With your every movement—
We are two—in step
With the beat of our hearts!

Fairy tales, Starlight, Shining Bright!
Underneath the moon of night—
Armor of Love
Armor of Knight
We—two—shall become—one—

In unison we glide—
Lifting our wings—
Discovering new and wondrous things,
Spreading twinkling dust
In commitment, faith, and trust!

Yes, my Super Hero! My Strength!
My hand is yours—to have and to hold.
This Angel is yours!
To love and adore!
I give you my hand, my heart, my eternal Love
And all the respect you deserve!

I love you,
Your Tinkerbell

True Love

Love fills a lifetime
and a lifetime begins this hour
when the two of us
Linda Beck
And
Randy Jones
begin a new life together
on Saturday, the twenty-seventh of November
at eleven o'clock in the morning
First Christian Church
Reidsville Highway
Glennville, Georgia

No sooner met, but they looked;
no sooner looked, but they loved;
no sooner loved, but they sighed;
no sooner sighed, but they asked one another the reason;
no sooner knew the reason, but they sought the remedy;
and in these degrees have they made
a pair of stairs to marriage. . . .

WILLIAM SHAKESPEARE
As You Like It
Act V, Scene II

Refuge

Steve and Pam Bianco

Good evening, Mr. Adams." Eighteen-year-old Steve Bianco greeted his date's father. "I'm here to pick up Pam."

"Come in, Steve. I believe I know you. Didn't we meet at a Boy Scout function last winter? You're an Eagle Scout, right?"

Pam walked into the room about that time, ready for her fourth date with Steve. "Hi, Steve."

"Hi, Pam. Yes, Mr. Adams. I was at that function. I remember seeing you as well."

"And now you're going out with my daughter. What happened to the blond you were with?"

Steve blushed furiously. "Excuse me? What blond?"

Mr. Adams laughed. "I'm just teasing you, son."

Pam shook her head as she led Steve out the door. "He's always doing things like that, Steve. You'll have to ignore him."

Pam Adams and Steve Bianco had begun dating just two days after seventeen-year-old Pam graduated from high school.

"But I've known you for a long time," Steve told Pam later. "Remember when you worked at the grocery store?"

"Yeah. . ."

"Remember when Richard asked you out?"

"Yeah. . ."

"And he was nearly four hours late?"

"He drove up with the car stereo blasting. I remember my dad answered the door and said that I couldn't go out with him. He never asked me out again."

Steve grinned. "I know. I intentionally kept him busy, which made him late, and was actually in the car with him. I'm the one who had the stereo up so loud."

"Steve, I know that you and Richard are best friends, but why did you do that?"

"I knew he wasn't right for you. I was. But I just had to wait. . .you know. . .for the right time."

It was a year after the "date that didn't happen" that Pam and Steve "officially" met at a party. During the party, Steve asked Pam if he could take her for a drive. Pam accepted and the two headed out for a moonlit drive in Steve's Toyota Landcruiser to Peavine Mountain in the Nevada Sierras. The top was down and the air was cold and breezy.

"The sky is huge tonight," Pam commented with a light shiver.

"Are you cold?"

Pam nodded. "A little. I didn't bring a coat."

Steve immediately slipped out of his. "Here. Take mine."

For the rest of the evening Steve and Pam quietly talked about everything and anything as they stared at the vast expanse of stars. Pam thought it was the most romantic ride of her life.

The romance didn't stop there. Being the true gentleman, Steve didn't kiss Pam until their third date. For the next eighteen months they dated. Chivalrous Steve often brought flowers to Pam.

One late afternoon Pam and her mother were talking in the kitchen of their home, waiting for Steve to arrive. When the doorbell rang, Mr. Adams answered the door and escorted Steve into the kitchen.

"What in the world?" Pam asked. Steve was carrying a long flower box with him.

"These are for you," he smiled shyly, extending the box.

Pam opened them, exposing the most beautiful long-stem red roses a girl would ever hope to possess. "They're beautiful!" she exclaimed as she shifted them slightly. As she did, a large diamond surrounded by a smaller diamond and an oval ruby winked at her from the stem of one of the roses. "Oh, my goodness! Steve!"

Steve never had a chance to say a word. Pam slipped the ring off the rose and onto her ring finger. Her mother was speechless. Her father patted Steve on the back and exclaimed, "It's about time!"

Steve and Pam married on November 21, 1981. Her wedding band has a corresponding smaller diamond and oval ruby, giving the rings the appearance of a flower.

Recently, as Pam reflected on the drive up to the mountain with Steve, she thought, *That could have been incredibly dangerous. You hardly knew him then!*

But she knows him now. According to Pam, Steve was and still is the safest refuge a girl can have.

Happy is the bride the sun shines on.

The belief in France was that the bride's clothes were lucky. Guests of the wedding would tear her dress as a keepsake. In order to protect their beautiful gowns, the brides began a tradition of throwing things of their choosing to the guests, including their garters. Though stockings requiring garters are not predominant today, the tradition of throwing the garter continues.

Her Knight in Shining Levi's

H. A. and Jan Northington

Jan App carefully folded the computer paper banner she hoped would soon be used. "If H. A. asks me to marry him," she said to her three- and five-year-olds, "then the answer will be right here on Mommy's banner."

Three weeks went by. One hot July morning, in a house on Wilton Drive in Cambria, California, Jan woke up and began the typical day of a single mother. She changed a wet bed, bathed and dressed her children, cleaned up spilled milk, and then headed outside to weed the backyard garden. The voice of her boyfriend of five months stopped her in her chores. "Jan, would you come out front?"

Jan stood, brushed the dirt from her hands and knees, then walked through the gate and stopped short. There stood H. A. holding the reins of a beautiful white horse.

Jan immediately recalled an evening, several months earlier, when she had jokingly informed H. A., "I've put out carrots and sugar cubes every night for the past two years. . .just waiting for my knight in shining armor to ride up on a white horse!"

Now, here he was.

"I've come to take you for a ride," he announced. "Hop on!"

Jan laughed. "Oh, it's my knight in shining Levi's!" she exclaimed. "But my children are inside. . .I can't. . ."

"Yes, you can," H.A. said without allowing Jan to finish her concern. "My boss is inside with them now."

Jan mounted the horse with H. A. "You thought of everything, huh?" With a quiet command, the horse began to walk down the street.

Just as they rounded the street corner, H. A. leaned back and said, "Well, I guess you can figure out what I am going to do. I am asking you to marry me."

Jan smiled. "The answer to that question is back home."

H. A. stopped the horse. "What! You mean to tell me I'm proposing to you on a white horse and you don't have an answer for me?"

"I'm telling you that your answer is back home," Jan insisted.

H. A. turned the horse about-face and commanded him to gallop.

As soon as they arrived in front of the house on Wilton Drive, (where H. A.'s boss was waiting outside with the children and a camera), Jan dismounted and ran into the house.

"Kids! Hurry! Help Mommy hold the banner!"

Ethan and Brittany stopped their play and quickly joined their mother in the front yard. Together the threesome pulled the banner from one end of the yard to the other. H. A. read:

> MY ANSWER IS (PICK ONE):
> 1. DEFINITELY
> 2. WITHOUT A DOUBT
> 3. OF COURSE
> 4. CERTAINLY
> 5. ABSOLUTELY
> 6. ALL OF THE ABOVE

A look of relief fell across H. A.'s handsome face. "Six! I pick number six!"

Later that evening H. A. shared how surprised he had been at Jan's initial answer. "When we were headed back to your house, I was thinking, 'Well, I thought I knew her. Is she going to have some contract or something for me to sign? If she does, I'm not sure I'm going for that!' For a while there I was afraid I didn't know you very well at all!"

Jan laughed. "You know me plenty well. I'm so glad I put out those carrots and sugar cubes for so long. . .it sure paid off!"

Jan and H. A. married one month later, on August 10, 1985.

*M*arry in September's shine,
Your living will be rich and fine.
If in October you do marry,
Love will come by riches tarry.
If you wed in bleak November,
Only joy will come, remember,
When December's showers fall fast,
Marry and true love will last.

*J*ust seeing you walk toward me on Friday night made my blood tingle and my skin tighten as though I had just seen a miracle from God, which in fact to me it was.

CORRADO RUFFONI to the woman who would one day be his wife, PAMELA MOORE (1943)

The Dairy Farmer

Alvin and Edna Mast

*I*n June 1936 both Alvin and Edna were in their early twenties. Alvin was the oldest son of a dairy farmer; Edna was an office worker in a nearby city. For several years they dated off and on. In the past year it had been more on than off.

"Edna, would you like to come to the farm for a weekend?" Alvin asked. "My family has extended an invitation for you to come."

Edna smiled warmly. "That'd be nice. I could use some time to relax. . .to get away from the city."

The weekend visit with Alvin's family was all that Edna hoped it would be. On Saturday evening, after a delicious home-cooked meal with his family, Alvin suggested, "Let's go for a walk."

"Okay."

Hand in hand Alvin and Edna strolled down a country road that cut through the center of the farm. Their only companions were the cattle who grazed on either side of them.

"I smell honeysuckle," Edna observed as she inhaled deeply.

Alvin pointed to the banks of both sides of the road. "The vines are everywhere around here."

"They sure smell good."

Suddenly Alvin stopped his walk and Edna stopped, too. Looking deeply into her eyes, he said, "Will you marry me and share with me the joys and sorrows of life?"

Time stood still then whirled around the young couple like a cyclone.

"Yes," Edna said and time resumed.

December 23, 1936, the young couple became one. In 1999 they celebrated their sixty-third wedding anniversary.

A Tryst in June

The honeysuckle—
A parasite indeed,
It tangles fence rows
And becomes a pesky weed.
But to a man and wife
Past three score and ten,
The fragrance of its bloom
Recalls the time when
On a June night
More than a half century ago,
He asked for her love
And she couldn't say, "No."

EDNA MAST

Fortune Cookie

Brad and Linda Vanderpool

As Linda Franklin and Brad Vanderpool were leaving the restaurant where they were dining with friends, Linda leaned over and confided, "Brad and I are talking about getting married."

"What! I thought the two of you were, as you so often put it, 'just friends'!"

Linda smiled. "I know. . .don't tell anyone, though. We'll see what happens."

"What happens" occurred over the next seven days, countdown

203

to Valentine's Day 1988. During that week, Linda, a school-teacher at Mary McPherson School in Meridian, Idaho, received a card a day from her boyfriend, Brad Vanderpool. Linda had met Brad at church while they were both attending Northwest Nazarene College where they were both actively involved in a singles group and in various musical ministries.

Brad and Linda had never "singled each other out." They were simply two people in a large singles group. After graduation Linda began teaching in Nampa (where the college is located). Brad graduated two years later and accepted a job teaching music in Hagerman, a small town about three hours south of Nampa. Over the next five years, Brad would visit Nampa for Homecoming, and Linda. . .but just "as friends."

After his five years in Hagerman, Brad moved to Portland, Oregon, and began working with his father in his family business. Portland and Nampa are four hundred miles apart, so seeing each other with any regularity was difficult.

In 1985 Brad called Linda with an invitation. "Hey! My church is going on a Caribbean cruise—there are about ten singles going—and I thought it would be fun for you, too. Would you be interested in going?"

"I don't know, Brad. Let me think about it."

Linda thought about it. The final verdict was a decision to go.

The cruise was fun; still there wasn't a romantic involvement between Brad and Linda. But that was 1985. Now it was 1988, and the two "friends" were very aware that their friendship had bloomed into something more.

On Friday, February 12, 1988, as Linda taught her fifth grade class, a knock came on the door. When she opened it, she was presented with a dozen red roses from her long-distance beau.

Linda was expecting Brad for dinner later that evening. When he arrived at the door to her home, he was met with soft romantic music, a blazing fire in the fireplace, scented candles illuminating the room, a delicious homemade dessert prepared by loving hands, and the roses on prominent display.

After greeting each other with a kiss, but before they sat down to dinner, Brad led Linda to her sofa. "I want to show you something," Brad said, then reached into a bag he had brought with him. He extracted a stack of letters.

"Are those letters?"

"Special letters. The first ones are from my grandfather. Here, read this," he instructed as he unfolded an aging piece of stationery.

" 'Dear Brad,' " Linda began. " 'For years now I have been praying for you. . .and for that special someone who will "make your pancakes." ' " Linda smiled. "How sweet."

"Some of the envelopes are addressed *To You and Yours.*"

"Precious."

"These next letters are from my pastor and friends in Portland."

Linda laughed lightly. "What do they say?"

"They're recommendations as to why you should marry me. Look at this one." Brad pulled from the stack a card cut in the shape of a VW Bug.

Linda began to read. " 'Linda, you should marry Brad because he has not previously been around the block, he is tuned to perfection, and his stereo system is the finest.' " They both laughed.

When Brad and Linda finished reading the letters, Brad pulled a fortune cookie out from the bag. "Open it," he said quietly.

Linda complied. As the cookie crumbled into several pieces, she recovered the little slip of paper that fell to her lap. "Accept the next proposition that you hear," she read as Brad slipped off the sofa and went down on one knee.

Linda's heart began to pound. He wasn't waiting until Valentine's Day; he was surprising her with an early proposal!

"Linda, will you marry me?" Brad asked.

"Yes!"

The newly betrothed couple sealed their commitment with a kiss. Linda picked up the fortune from the cookie and gazed at it. "Isn't this the same fortune I got in a cookie a couple of months ago when you and I went out for Chinese?"

Brad smiled. "Yeah. I picked it up from the table as we were leaving, then very carefully slipped it into the cookie you just opened."

A month later, Linda decided to reinforce the answer she had given Brad that Friday before Valentine's Day. She sent him a one-pound fortune cookie, dipped in dark and white chocolate, with a fortune that simply read, "YES!"

Guests at a Polish wedding buy a dance with the bride. This money is used to help pay for the honeymoon.

Darling wife, I have a number of requests to make to you: —First, I beg you will not be melancholy. Second, that you will take care of yourself and not expose yourself to the spring breezes. Third, that you will not go out to walk alone—indeed, it would be better not to walk at all. Fourth, that you will feel entirely assured of my love.

WOLFGANG AMADEUS MOZART

Isn't He Wonderful?

Scott and Stefanie Parnell

*C*an you believe that if you or I had lived just two streets west or two streets south, we would have gone to school together?" Stefanie Scherer asked her boyfriend of exactly one year as they drove to the home of his grandparents. That day Scott's family would be celebrating his grandmother's birthday, and Scott had convinced Stefanie to drive the one hundred miles from Bethany, Oklahoma, to Dill City, Oklahoma.

"Small world," Scott replied. "Point is, we did meet up finally."

Stefanie shifted slightly as she adjusted the khaki shorts Scott had requested she wear to the family outing. She looked out the window and thought how odd his request had been.

Stefanie couldn't help but be a little put out with Scott that warm, May afternoon. It was their anniversary, and Scott's parents were in Dill City. Because the two of them both lived at home (keeping Scott and Stefanie from ever having any alone time), she had hoped that after church and a celebration lunch at their favorite restaurant they could rent a movie and watch it at Scott's family home. But Scott had insisted that the two of them drive to Dill City for the birthday dinner with his family. Stranger still, he had insisted that they change their church clothes and that Stefanie wear her khaki shorts and denim shirt with cowboys stitched on it. Scott, on the other hand, was wearing old jeans and a t-shirt.

A little over an hour later, Scott and Stefanie arrived at the farm of Scott's grandparents where they were met by his maternal grandparents and his mother and father. No sooner had they arrived than Scott and his father announced that they were going to make a quick trip to Scott's uncle's farm just down the road.

"I'll go with you," Stefanie said.

"No, no. You stay here and talk with Mom and my grand-parents."

A half an hour passed. Scott's father, Bob, returned to the house but without Scott. "Scott stayed down at his uncle's house," Stefanie was told. "Why don't you and Phyllis and I go down there as well and visit?"

Stefanie dutifully got in the truck with Scott's parents and proceeded down the dirt road that led to the uncle's farm. Conversation was nonexistent until Scott's father pulled into a gravel driveway and stopped the car. Turning to Stefanie, he said, "You need to get out here."

Stefanie's brow furrowed. "What?"

"Just trust me, Stefanie. You need to get out here."

As Stefanie opened the truck's door, she noted that Scott's mother was sliding out of the cab behind her.

"Get back in the truck, Phyllis," Bob said.

"I want to see," Phyllis said quietly. To Stefanie the voices seemed to be coming through a tunnel. *Surely,* she thought, *this was just something special that Scott had devised for their anniversary.*

"Get back in the truck," Bob repeated. "Stefanie, walk around that tree there in front of us and you'll know where to go from there." The cab door was shut and Scott's parents drove away.

Stefanie stepped around the large tree as she was told. On the other side were a bench and a small birdbath. On the bench was Scott's Bible, opened to 1 Corinthians 13, the "love chapter." Across his Bible lay a dozen red roses. In front of the bench was a quilt all spread out with what appeared to be a million rose petals scattered on top of it. Scott was nowhere to be found.

In the distance, the sound of thunder seemed to come from the rich earth. Stefanie recognized it as a horse's gallop, moving closer and closer to where she stood. She peered around the tree and saw Scott riding on a horse toward her. He was no longer wearing the old jeans and t-shirt. He now wore nice jeans, a white dress shirt, and his white cowboy hat.

He is a vision! Stefanie thought as Scott brought the horse to a stop and got down off the horse. "Stefanie, come sit down over here on the bench," he said.

Stefanie walked back to the bench and sat. Scott joined her, then got down on one knee. Stefanie could see him shaking from nervousness and could hear the quiver in his voice as he spoke. "Stefanie, I may not be a knight in shining armor, but I promise to love you forever. Will you be my wife?"

Stefanie threw her arms around Scott. "Yes! Yes! Yes! I can't believe you want to marry me! Yes!"

Scott and Stefanie chose January 8, 1999, as their wedding date, mainly because the date coincided with their Christmas break from University of Central Oklahoma where they were both students. Unfortunately, this day was the only day of "winter" Oklahoma City experienced. The entire city was a sheet of ice. Because their wedding was scheduled for seven o'clock that evening, the wedding party spent the day sliding around town, getting Stefanie's hair done, and picking up her father's tuxedo.

"This is very nearly a nightmare," Stefanie exclaimed to Scott at 5:30 that morning after being told that family members and bridesmaids were stranded en route.

"As long as you, me, and the preacher are there, it will all be fine."

Stefanie took in a deep breath and sighed. *Isn't he wonderful?* she thought.

I fear for what we are doing.
Are you sure you shall love me forever?
Shall we never repent?
I fear and I hope.

LADY MARY PIERREPOINT
to her husband
on the night of their elopement, 1712

The Wonderful World
of Disney

Jim and Jamie-Lynn Santee

I don't really feel like going back on tour," professional ice skater Jamie-Lynn Kitching told her mother just two months after her father had passed away on May 4, 1984. "But Dad knew how much I loved to skate, and I know he would want me to continue with my passion."

Jamie-Lynn's mother wrapped her arms around her daughter. "Yes, he would. I'm sure you'll do all right. As soon as you begin practice again, and get on the road, you'll find the days easier to bear. It's good to have something to occupy your time."

Jamie-Lynn left her home in Montreal, Canada, and headed for Lakeland, Florida, where skating rehearsals for Walt Disney's "Donald Duck's 50th Birthday Celebration on Ice" would soon begin. She had been with the show for two years and was warmly greeted by her fellow skaters. The last time she had seen them was just before her father had died. In spite of his being in the hospital, he had insisted that Jamie-Lynn fly to Florida for the scheduled advanced rehearsals and costume fitting.

"Guess who's joining the show?" she was asked by one of the show's members.

"I give up. Who?"

"Jim Santee. He was here last week. You missed meeting him."

"You're kidding! I've heard a lot about him! He's a great skater!"

"We're all pretty excited around here."

Jim Santee had been skating for twenty of his twenty-three years and had built for himself a fine reputation as a top skater. A few months later, when Jamie-Lynn returned to join the show, he and Jamie-Lynn became instant friends. As she continued to move through the difficult times surrounding her father's death, Jim became a godsend for her, emotionally.

Some time later, God showed Jamie-Lynn and Jim how His hand had worked in Jim's joining the show. As Jamie-Lynn went through some papers, she found the letter that had informed Jim of his being accepted in the show. "Look at the postmark on the envelope," Jamie-Lynn said to Jim.

Jim took the envelope. "May 4, 1984."

"The day my father died."

Making it even more special for Jamie-Lynn was the fact that her father's name was also Jim.

By December 1985, Jamie-Lynn and Jim had been dating and living out of suitcases for a year and a half. On the night before the December 29, 1985, matinee show, performed in Anaheim, California, Jamie-Lynn showed Jim a camcorder.

"Mom gave it to us for Christmas so that we can record our routines and critique them."

"What a great idea! I'm giving it to Sheldon so that he can

tape us tomorrow afternoon at the matinee show."

"Oh. Okay."

The next afternoon, at the end of the opening number, Jamie-Lynn—as the lead chimney sweep—and Jim—as a Russian Cossack dancer—skated side by side, center ice. As extra lighting poured upon the couple, Jim unexpectedly dropped to one knee. *What is this jokester up to now?* Jamie-Lynn thought. One look at his face, however, told her that she should pay attention. Jim moved to pull something away from his belt. That was when she noticed a ring in his hand. He took her hand in his and slipped the ring on her finger.

As the Seven Dwarfs, Mickey Mouse, Minnie Mouse, Donald Duck, and the rest of the gang stood around clapping, and a friend videotaped from the cheering audience, Jamie-Lynn and Jim gave each other a long hug.

On June 20, 1987, Jamie-Lynn and Jim married in the church her parents had married in twenty-five years earlier, St. Andrews Church, Thunder Bay, Ontario. As Jamie-Lynn the chimney sweep was surrounded by "friends" when Jim the Russian Cossack dancer proposed, Jamie-Lynn the bride was surrounded by her large and loving family when she said, "I do."

"Dear beast, you shall not die," said Beauty. "You will live in order to become my husband. From this moment on, I give you my hand and I swear that I shall be yours alone. Alas! I thought that I felt only friendship for you, but the sorrow that I feel now makes me see that I cannot live without you!" MADAME LEPRINCE DE BEAUMONT
from *Beauty and the Beast;*
translation by ALFRED and MARY ELIZABETH DAVID

Cake, grain, fruit, sweetmeats, flowers, petals,
confetti, shoes, rice, and birdseed
have all been used to throw at the bride and groom. . .
symbols of fertility.

Easter Eggs and Baskets

Patrick and Sheila Aland

Patrick Aland knew he wanted to marry Sheila Levi after only two months of dating. Sheila felt the same. Love hit hard and fast, but the two college students were smart enough to realize that education should come first; marriage would follow soon enough.

After a year, Patrick was ready to pop the question. "I'm thinking about putting together an Easter basket for Sheila," he told his mother. "Somehow I'll put the ring in the basket. . .hide it."

"That sounds like fun! And it's a very good idea. Where'd you come up with it?"

Patrick shrugged. "I don't know, really. I knew I wanted to ask her on a special event, like a holiday, and Easter seems like a good time to do it. As far as the basket, I knew I wanted it to be original and I've never really heard of anyone doing this, so. . .I wanted to talk to her father in person, but I'm going to have to call him and talk with him over the phone. It's not the way I want to do it, but with him living an hour or so from here, I won't have the opportunity to see him before Easter."

Patrick made the phone call. "I love Sheila very much," he began. "And I want to ask her to marry me on Easter Sunday."

Sheila's father was receptive to the idea. "Well, I'd be very happy for both of you," he said.

The Saturday before Easter Sunday, Patrick put Sheila's Easter basket together: a potpourri of chocolate marshmallow bunnies, chewing gum, jellybeans, and a large chocolate bunny. Finally, he opened a purple plastic egg, filled it with candy, then slipped the ring in the center before closing it and placing it in the middle of the basket. With great anticipation, he hid the basket so that Sheila wouldn't find it early.

On Easter Sunday Patrick presented Sheila with the basket.

"Oh, how cute!" she exclaimed, then sat on the sofa and placed the basket in her lap. Patrick sat next to her and his smile faded to a frown. He expected her to go right for the big egg, but she didn't. Instead, she rummaged through everything else. "Let's see what we have here. . .chocolate bunny. . .that's original. . .some gum, some jellybeans. . .marshmallow bunnies. . . . Is there anything in the plastic egg?" She picked up the egg. Patrick wondered if she could hear his heart thumping in his chest. A knot formed in his throat and he smiled.

The plastic egg was popped open, revealing multicolored candy. The ring had slipped slightly from its place and was not openly visible. A manicured fingernail thumped through the candy. A gasp escaped from Sheila's lips and she turned and threw her arms around Patrick.

"Sheila, will you marry me?" Patrick asked formally.

"Yes!" Sheila said. "Yes!"

*L*et us rejoice and be glad and give him glory!
For the wedding of the Lamb has come,
and his bride has made herself ready.

REVELATION 19:7 NIV

*For this reason a man will
leave his father and mother
and be united to his wife,
and the two will become one flesh."
This is a profound mystery—
but I am talking about Christ and the church.*

EPHESIANS 5:31–32 NIV

Our Wedding Day

Best Man: _____

_____

Groomsmen: _____

_____

_____

Ring Bearer: _____

Maid of Honor: _____

Matron of Honor: _____

Bridesmaids: _____

_____

_____

Junior Bridesmaids: _____

_____

_____

Flower Girl: _____

Special Guests: _____

Songs That Were Played: _____

Songs That Were Sung: _____

Special Words That Were Spoken: _____

_____

_____

Personal Vows That Were Given:_____

_____

_____

Our Favorite Scripture(s): _____

Our Favorite Song: _____

Our Favorite Place to Go: _____

Our Favorite Restaurant: _____

Our Favorite Thing to Do: _____

Our Favorite Poem:_____

Our Favorite Quote:_____

Her Favorite Perfume: _____

His Favorite Aftershave/Cologne:_____

The Groom's Memoirs

1. What do you recall about the first time you saw the woman who would become your wife?

2. When did you know that you wanted to ask her out on a date?

3. Describe your first date from your perspective.

4. What was the turning point in your relationship? How did you know that she was "the one"?

5. Describe buying the ring.

6. Did you ask her father for permission to marry his daughter? Describe what happened.

7. What special plans did you orchestrate for your proposal?

8. Had you discussed marriage beforehand? Were you certain she was going to say yes?

9. In your words, describe the proposal. What did you say? What did she say? Do you remember what she was wearing?

The Bride's Memoirs

1. What do you recall about the first time you saw the man who would become your husband?

2. What are your recollections of the first time he asked you out?

3. Describe your first date from your perspective.

4. What happened the first time he kissed you?

5. Describe a particular conversation that was memorable to you.

6. Were you suspicious that he was going to propose? Why or why not? If so, did you know how you were going to respond?

7. What are your special memories of the proposal? What was the date? What were the two of you wearing?

This Certifies

That on the _____ day

of _____ in the year of our Lord _____

_____

and

_____

were by me

United in Marriage at

_____

_____

according to the ordinance of God

and the Laws of _____

(State)

Signed: _____

A final Word:

I do not wish you joy without a sorrow,
Nor endless day without the healing dark,
Nor brilliant sun without the restful shadow,
Nor tides that never turn against your bark.
I wish you love, and strength, and wisdom,
And gold enough to help some needy one,
I wish you songs, but also blessed silence,
And God's sweet peace when every day is done.

UNKNOWN

About the Author

EVA MARIE EVERSON is an author, teacher, and speaker on a variety of subjects designed to develop intimate relationships with God. She writes for several ministries and publications, teaches Old Testament theology at Life Training Center in Orlando, Florida and is a contributing author for many books. Eva and her husband live in Orlando, have three children, and are expecting their first grandchild.

Eva Marie enjoys hearing from her readers and invites you to email her. The address is: BridegroomsBride@aol.com.